APPLAUSE FOR
MARATHON FAITH

"Having just run my first marathon, I have a new appreciation for the title and this book—*Marathon Faith*. We live in a culture that celebrates fifteen minutes of fame, but in God's kingdom, it's about long obedience in the same direction. *Marathon Faith* will inspire you to run longer and run stronger. Thanks to my friend, John Van Pay, for setting the pace!"

—**MARK BATTERSON**, bestselling author of *The Circle Maker* and lead pastor of National Community Church

"My friend, John Van Pay, has given us a wonderful gift in his book, *Marathon Faith*. He reminds us that living for Christ is an endurance race, not a sprint, and that it's not how we start, but whether we finish that counts. Drawing from the stories of real people in Hebrews 11—all of them as human and vulnerable as we are—this book bores into our souls with conviction, challenge, insight, humor and captivating storytelling. John is my daughter's pastor and a personal hero of mine, and I commend not only his book but also the integrity of who he is to you."

—**DR. JAMES BRADFORD**, general secretary of the United States Assemblies of God and author of *Lead So Others Can Follow*

"Every Christian has trouble in life and struggles with living out his or her faith. John Van Pay, a pastor and endurance athlete, has written a compelling book to encourage us not only to survive but also to run our races victoriously by the power of the Holy Spirit. *Marathon Faith* uses the flawed examples from Hebrews' Faith Hall of Fame to show us how God turns our weaknesses into durable strengths."

—**SCOTT WILSON**, pastor of The Oaks Fellowship Church and author of *Clear the Stage*

"Keeping pace, finding rhythm, and focusing on the prize are all things that help not only marathon runners but also everyone who is on the journey of life. *Marathon Faith* reminds us that Jesus is the best pace setter. It gives examples of real leaders from the Bible who will inspire you to not throw in the towel. Thanks, John, for helping so many discover the courage to live life with greater endurance."

—**DOUG CLAY**, general superintendent of the United States Assemblies of God

"Look at the table of contents. That's all it took for me. I want to be like all those named. They had one thing in common: they finished their lives well. I too want to finish well. In *Marathon Faith*, my friend, John Van Pay, says, you can. You must. I will. So can you."

—**SAMUEL CHAND**, leadership consultant and author of *Bigger, Faster Leadership*

"You can feel John's love for God leaping off these pages. *Marathon Faith* is more than a great read, it's a manual for running the race. John does an excellent job of articulating the stories of the great runners who have gone before us."

—**BILL TAYLOR**, chief meteorologist at KENS 5 Eyewitness News, San Antonio, Texas

"*Marathon Faith* presents an innovative "Faith" training program that is right on target. This is a very insightful book that is extremely beneficial for anyone seeking to increase their endurance in faith. John shares his personal stories, making it even more compelling. His experience and knowledge supports athletes and anyone seeking a real and lasting relationship with God. I highly recommend reading John's book and using it as a training tool to guide you through this amazing journey with Christ."

—**APRIL LEAL**, owner of Your Destination Fit and Christ follower

"Having known John for nearly thirty years, I have watched him live out the principles he shares in this book. John is not a quitter. Through tragedy and setbacks, John has persevered and kept his eye on the prize. As you read his story, you will be inspired to press on through your obstacles and FINISH your race! Thanks, John, for running your race with integrity and passion!"

—**BRIAN DOLLAR**, associate pastor of First Assembly Church, North Little Rock, Arkansas, and author of *I Blew It!* and *Talk Now and Later*

"In a time of ever increasing darkness in the world, there stands a remnant. This band of devoted disciples is wholeheartedly committed to the cause of Christ. One of the men serving Christ is John Van Pay. He has served in excellence for over three decades, declaring vision and deeply loving the people around him. *Marathon Faith* is an encouraging overview and exposition of Hebrews' hall of faith. John's ridiculously funny and encouraging stories drive home the eternal principles that will help you finish your race."

—**W. KYLE VOLKMER**, teaching pastor of Gateway Fellowship Church and author of *These Things*

"From years of pastoral experience, I've seen first-hand the pattern of people starting fast and hot in faith but becoming overwhelmed and flaming out over time. How can we as spiritual leaders help people finish the race of faith in a world full of challenges and difficulties? John Van Pay offers biblical solutions to real life struggles of faith in *Marathon Faith.* John is one of the most thoughtful and committed disciple makers I know, and he's built his life and church on the principles in this book. Whether you're starting your own race, or you've been running for a while, or you're helping others run their race of faith, you will no doubt find yourself motivated and inspired to go the next mile."

—**CHRIS RAILEY**, network director of the Church Multiplication Network for the United States Assemblies of God

"William Carey, when asked about the secret of his missionary success, said, 'I can plod. I can persevere in any definite pursuit. To this I owe everything.' Biblical faith is a blend of great expectations and great endurance. We believe God can do improbable, impossible, immediate things, AND we commit to arduous yet rewarding processes of trusting obedience. Using Scripture and story, John Van Pay shows how Christian life and service are enjoyable runs of endurance, plodding pleasures. As the global Church takes Jesus seriously in its obedience to "Finish the Task" by preaching the Gospel to every group of people, we are all going to need *Marathon Faith.*"

—**DICK BROGDEN**, founder of the Live Dead movement in Cairo, Egypt

MARATHON FAITH

MARATHON FAITH

MOTIVATION from the GREATEST ENDURANCE RUNNERS of the BIBLE

JOHN VAN PAY

REGNERY
FAITH

Cataloging-in-Publication data on file with the Library of Congress

ISBN 978-1-62157-677-8
e-book ISBN 978-1-62157-709-6

Published in the United States by
Regnery Faith
An Imprint of Regnery Publishing
A Division of Salem Media Group
300 New Jersey Ave NW
Washington, DC 20001
www.RegneryFaith.com

Manufactured in the United States of America

10 9 8 7 6 5 4 3 2 1

I dedicate this to my dearly loved children, Hannah Grace, Emma, and Bryce. You are my treasure. With every word, I thought of you in my mind and prayed for you from my heart. The Lord has a great purpose for your life, and I will do whatever it takes to help you fulfill it. May you finish your race to the glory of God.

I love you.

Daddy

CONTENTS

INTRODUCTION xiii

1 Look Where You Want to Go—JESUS 1

2 Die Daily—ABEL 13

3 Walk with God—ENOCH 25

4 Swing that Hammer—NOAH 39

5 Better Together—ABRAHAM and SARAH 53

6 Pass the Baton—ISAAC 67

7 Fight—JACOB 77

8 Trials Possess Great Purpose—JOSEPH 89

9 Be Brave—JOCHEBED 101

10 Know Who You Are—MOSES 113

11 All In—RAHAB 123

12 Drop the Dead Weight—GIDEON 133

13 Don't Let Success Get to Your Head—BARAK 145

14 Don't Let Failure Get to Your Heart—SAMSON 155

15 Grit—JEPHTHAH 165

16 Constant Forgiveness—DAVID 175

17 Rest to Be Your Best—SAMUEL 187

18 Persevering with Prayer—DANIEL 197

19 Amigos—SHADRACH, MESHACH, and ABEDNEGO 207

20 The Finish Line—YOU 217

ACKNOWLEDGMENTS 229

NOTES 231

INTRODUCTION

SURRENDERING YOUR LIFE to JESUS IS the BEGINNING of YOUR MARATHON LIFE of FAITH

Finishing is better than starting.

ECCLESIASTES 7:8, NLT

"I WILL NOT SWIM WITH THE SHARKS!"

My wife Stephanie faced her greatest fear lurking beneath her in the frigid, dark waters of the Gulf of Mexico. Uncomfortable and restricted by a wetsuit and paralyzed by fear on a sandy beach, she refused to start the swim section of her first triathlon. In that moment I knew I could only be successful as her coach if she trusted me, overcame her fear, and pushed onward to cross the finish line.

How will you respond when you face your greatest obstacle and everything in you screams to quit? Your life is your race. You were created to run it, but realize running the race is not easy. It isn't a sprint; it's a marathon. Finishing strong requires an attitude of tough endurance. It's not something you were born with, and it doesn't come free. Scripture doesn't say finishing requires talent, speed, good looks, a boatload of cash, or even happiness but an attitude of tough endurance, and that endurance comes through suffering and overcoming obstacles.

I pray this book will help you discover the essentials from the endurance runners of the Bible. Did you realize the Bible mentions 3,237 different people? Of the approximately 1,300 spiritual leaders from Scripture, on average, only one in three finished well. You will learn in my favorite chapters of the Bible, Hebrews 11 and 12, that the endurance runners are not listed to cheer you on. It's what you will see in them that makes the difference in your race. None are perfect. None are better than the rest of us. Abel had sibling issues. Noah loved wine too much. Abraham lied. Jacob deceived. Moses murdered. Samson loved himself some women. David struggled with all of the above. They were jacked up and so are we. The one thing they possessed was endurance. Faith made them strong. "By faith" is listed twenty-seven times in Hebrews 11 alone.

Grit is missing today when things get tough. I believe God called me to write this book because I'm broken over those I love who quit early. It's not okay that many ministers who start well are taken out right before their breakthrough, or that students who graduate soon quit following the Lord. So many start a journey of following Jesus without a realistic expectation of the price required to finish their spiritual race. As a result, they get frustrated and lose spiritual passion for Jesus.

Anyone can toe the line, but not everyone will endure to the end. A follower of Jesus is not called to sit on the sofa and binge watch another television series. It's an endurance race. When your body is done and your emotional tank is empty, what remains? Your race will be relentless. It requires discipline, difficult training, sacrifice, the ability to suffer, and an enduring faith. Hebrews

11:1–2 says, "Now faith is the assurance of things hoped for, the conviction of things not seen. For by it the people of old received their commendation." The endurance runners listed in this book possessed a faith certain of the reality of God. Do you have this endurance that will do whatever it takes to finish? It's your choice. If you quit early, it's on you. If you finish, all glory belongs to the Lord.

How can you develop endurance? How can you not quit in the face of hardship and pain? Acquiring the wisdom needed to develop endurance comes from applying the experience of others. In every chapter, you will discover a new endurance runner listed in Hebrews 11. You will be inspired by stories and practical lessons that will help you become a finisher. Unlike you, the endurance runners passed away before Jesus came and didn't witness the fulfillment of the greatest promise. But they're with Him now and waiting for you to join them. The great cloud is incomplete without you. To join them and finish well you must lock your eyes on our Lord Jesus Christ. He persevered through every obstacle, trial, and temptation. You can too by learning from His perfect example. You can also learn from the mistakes of others, myself included. After doing twenty-five years of ministry and finishing seventy endurance events, I discovered important principles to help you succeed.

You will fail more times than you can count, but you must get back up and continue. So much is at stake. You will face obstacles. They are the trials and temptations keeping you from finishing your race. Health problems. Relational conflict. Past failure. Shame. Marriage issues. Work problems. Financial storms. It may seem impossible to overcome. There is a real enemy who is like a shark waiting to take you out. This enemy desires to steal, kill, and destroy you. Don't be afraid. It won't be easy. Don't raise the white flag. Never quit. You are not alone. God is for you. Never believe the lie that you don't have what it takes to finish. Discover the essentials found in Jesus and the endurance runners who've gone before you to help you reach the finish line. Jesus said in this world you will have troubles, but take heart because He has overcome the world.

This book will challenge you to last. The race begins at a new birth in Christ Jesus. It ends at the finish line when you fulfill His greatest purpose. I hope this book flips your switch. There is a prize at the finish line. It's not a medal or a first-place trophy. Those will rust and crumble. The prize at your finish line will bring you more joy than you could ever imagine. Dig deep. You are stronger than you think. Discover the courage Jesus instills in you. Find comfort in knowing you're not alone in your mistakes.

You may not have to finish everything you start, but you must finish what is most important. This book will train you to overcome common obstacles. You are living in a critical time. Now more than ever, you need to realize you can't run this race on your own. As Stephanie trusted me to be her coach, trust God to use this book as a training tool to help you overcome what you will face.

It comes down to three simple words: FINISH YOUR RACE. Turn the pages, and let's run it together.

"Let us run with endurance the race God has set before us" (Hebrews 12:1).

1

LOOK WHERE YOU WANT TO GO

JESUS

Jesus + Nothing = Everything

THE ROAD SEEMED TO STRETCH LONGER AND LONGER AS I pushed one pedal down after the other. As I rode my bike up to the traffic light on the feeder of I-40 in middle-of-nowhere, Arkansas, I lost the little strength I needed to simply pull my cleats out of the clips in my pedals. With my feet stuck to my pedals, you can imagine what happened next.

I collapsed, crashing into the pavement. The pain of biting hunger and road rash caused by the fall kept me on my back. I only had nine miles left ahead. Did I have what it would take to get back up and finish the race? I cycled 301 miles from Fort Smith to West Memphis in twenty-three hours and needed to embrace my "why" if I was to continue. While lying on the hot asphalt, my eyes found the small portrait of a missionary in China I had taped to the stem of my bike before beginning the race. I remembered the sacrifice he was making away from his family to care for orphans and the risk he was taking to share his faith "underground" in a closed, oppressed country. I promised him I would finish. Donors gave thousands of dollars to this charity ride so he could have a new van to spread the Gospel. Remembering my "why" was essential to digging deep, finding the strength, and getting back on my bike to finish the race.

The last few miles of every long-distance race are the most difficult, especially when you hit the wall as I did. No matter your preparation, every endurance runner is tempted to quit. It becomes the defining moment when you discover who you really are. You question if it's worth it. The temptation to quit is like a sabotaging thread woven through your purpose, relationships, job, and life. The voice to quit becomes deafening. It says, "cut the corner," "leave early," "I don't need this," "raise the white flag," or even "just move on." It's not how you start or how fast you run, but how you finish the race that counts. When you are tempted over and over to give up, it's essential to remember your "why." Why do you do the things you do and for whom do you do them? You will need your "why" for the hell to come.

The dramatic but telling play-by-play of that pivotal moment when I faced defeat head-on pales in comparison to my friend who was a little younger than me when he completed his own long-distance race.

No one believed he could finish. His closest friends and family begged him not to go. Even though he considered an alternative route, once he crossed that starting line he set his mind to never quit until he finished the race.

The crowd never cheered. Instead they jeered at him and screamed for him to fail, to fall under the crushing weight of ever-increasing pain and the walls still to come. Instead of a helmet of protection, he was given a thorny crown to pierce his brow. Instead of Gatorade, they spit in his face. Instead of an energy gel for a needed burst of strength, they whipped him with their words. They laughed and mocked without mercy. A 125-pound burden was strapped to the back of his shoulders. Dirt mixed with sweat and blood clouded his vision.

And yet one foot continued to step in front of the other.

In the final stretch of his race, even the taunting crowd cringed at the repeating strikes of a cruel hammer producing the worst pain a human could endure. Every breath brought searing pain as he pushed his feet down against an unyielding spike. It tore muscle, tendon, and bone. To cross his finish line, he would have to give everything he had: his life.

It is finished.

No one took the life of Jesus. He laid it down at the finish line. The author of Hebrews explains in the twelfth chapter that Jesus endured the cross for the joy set before Him. What could possibly bring joy powerful enough to finish the hardest race man ever ran? Jesus never forgot His why. His why behind the cross was love. The prophetic words of Jesus came true in John 15:13: "Greater love has no one than this, that someone lay down his life for his friends." His love was the why that brought glory to His father by fulfilling God's will to bring about your salvation. Jesus suffered the greatest pain anyone would ever endure. Jesus loved you that much.

All believers need encouragement in the face of what may seem like insurmountable odds. The early Church, during the first century when the Book of Hebrews was written, experienced such a time. The letter to the Hebrews was written for two reasons. First, to encourage us to never quit because of the pressure exerted from circumstances, those around us, or our own failings and pasts. It was written to recently converted Jews of that time. These Christians lived under constant persecution and pressure, not only from the world but also from friends and family, to return to their former way of life and the religion of Judaism. The second reason was a reminder that Jesus is greater. The author of Hebrews knew these Christians only needed to know Jesus and their resolve would be set.

> Therefore, since we are surrounded by so great a cloud of witnesses, let us also lay aside every weight, and sin which clings so closely, and let us run with endurance the race that is set before us, looking to Jesus, the founder and perfecter of our faith, who for the joy that was set before him endured the cross, despising the shame, and is seated at the right hand of the throne of God. Consider him who endured from sinners such hostility against himself, so that you may not grow weary or fainthearted (Hebrews 12:1–3).

The cloud of witnesses is not the focus on which our heart is fixed. The Greek word for "witness" is actually "martyr." A martyr is one who never renounces what he or she believes, even under persecution. He or she never quits.

You will discover more about these endurance runners in later chapters, but for now choose where you will fix your own eyes. Not on the many who went before you but the One. Instead of including Jesus in the heroes of faith in chapter eleven, He stands apart. No one compares. All others are a distant second at best. When your gaze is fixed on Jesus first, above all others, you will discover the foundational strength needed to complete your own journey of faith. Your "why" must be an unselfish love and obedience to our Lord Jesus Christ. Carefully examine and commit to memory how Jesus set his mind to never, ever quit, even in the face of insurmountable odds. Jesus endured everything thrown at Him. His endurance becomes your fortitude. When you are tempted to quit early, never forget to return your gaze to the story of the ultimate finisher. To Jesus.

Look where you want to go. All trail runners and mountain bikers have discovered that if you let a rock or tree root psyche you out, you'll stare at it and hit it every time. Look for the clean line and hold it. Once, our pastors took a multi-day, twenty-six-mile canoe trip through the beautiful Santa Elena Canyon in Big Bend National Park. It should be on every paddler's bucket list. The most technical, class three, white water section of the Rio Grande River is called Rock Slide Rapids. You must canoe through a maze of boulders bigger than a house. My partner was our student ministry pastor whom I affectionately call Griz. We made a commitment to each other never to look at a boulder no matter how nice it was. We took a deep breath and were quickly thrust into the maze. Whenever a mammoth boulder was near, I would yell, "Keep paddling. Keep paddling." A huge rush of satisfaction and relief comes when you navigate the Rock Slide cleanly. If you go first, you have the luxury of looking back with guilty pleasure when your friend's canoe tips. Watch the show. Don't be the show. Look where you want to go. The three common perception problems on your spiritual race are the following: no view of Jesus, a distorted view of Jesus, or a low view of Jesus.

NO VIEW OF JESUS

Most of the time it's not blindness but fixating on the wrong thing. What gets your attention gets you. Jesus says in Matthew 6:22, "The eye is the lamp of the body. So, if your eye is healthy, your whole body will be full of light." Is your body dark because your eye is unhealthy?

When you have abundance, it's tempting to be self-reliant and have no desire for a savior. You become God in your life, and all your focus revolves around your needs, wants, and dreams. Quitting has less to do with self-reliance and more to do with what you've forgotten about the character and nature of God. One of the greatest temptations is to fashion God in your own image. You default to worshiping a god of your own character and preference. Instead of believing and trusting man is created in God's image, you become guilty of breaking the first commandment—making a god after your own image. It's idolatry. You can't make God in your own image.

Anything or anyone who gets more devotion than Jesus is an idol. Evaluate the time you give your favorite sports team, hobby, work, social media, or even ministry, friends, and family. Where does your mind drift while you are lying in bed at night, taking a shower, or waking in the morning? It isn't a passion problem. It's where you direct your passion. If you love the Church or a worship song more than the person of Jesus, you have a real problem. You are missing out. What if you redirected your focus to Jesus? What if He became the single greatest object of your attention? "But seek first the kingdom of God and his righteousness, and all these things will be added to you" (Matthew 6:33).

DISTORTED VIEW OF JESUS

The popular worldview today is that you will reach God no matter what trail you choose in your spiritual journey. If you disagree, you are intolerant and filled with hate. The very people who once preached tolerance and accused Christians of being intolerant bigots only a few decades ago have become intolerant themselves. Now that they have achieved a level of cultural acceptance, "tolerance" is thrown out the window. Under the pressure of such hatred and persecution, Christians have begun to let their moral stance and belief in the absolute truth of the Word of God slide. But the Church's dangerous shift is less about conforming ourselves into the image of the world and more about what we've forgotten about God.

What makes Jesus unique is He came down the mountain because of His love for you. John 1:14 says, "the Word became flesh and dwelt among us." He humbled Himself from a position in heaven, came down to personally reveal the character and nature of God, and then died for you. There are many wonderful people to be respected and admired in Scripture and Church history, but only One is worthy of worship. Although many have tried to worship other gods and people, no one has been so wonderfully loved as Jesus. Jesus said, "I am the way, and the truth, and the life. No one comes to the Father except through me" (John 14:6).

Who or what sits on the throne of your heart as God? You must know who God is based on the Bible, not on the constantly shifting misconceptions thrown around by the changing times and the loudest voices in our culture. If you see God as a genie in a bottle, you will be frustrated when He doesn't answer your prayers according to your preferences. If you see Him as a cosmic cop, you will be constantly looking over your shoulder after every mistake. If you see Him as distant because you have a dysfunctional relationship with your earthly father, you will never have the personal relationship He desires to have with you. Every misconception produces dangerous consequences. Studying the nature of God as revealed through Jesus in your Bible will help you see the one true God. Christ walked among men to show who God really is. He faced every trial and temptation you will face. He can say, "Me too." His words and actions flowed from His character. His attributes will shape you. You become what you behold. Your actions and words will flow from a right view of God. Trust the character of God. Trust in His promises.

LOW VIEW OF JESUS

The inner circle of Jesus was told by God not to look around but to keep its gaze on Jesus. Peter wanted to build three altars on top of the mountain where Jesus was transfigured with Moses and Elijah. God commanded this inner circle to only listen to His beloved Son. Only Jesus is the author and finisher of your faith. Only Jesus is your hope. Only Jesus will enable you to cross your finish line. Looking back will cause you to stumble. Looking down will bring discouragement. Looking around will make you feel inferior. Your prize is not a what, it's a Who. When you discover this, it will shoot joy and renewed strength through your veins.

> Long ago, at many times and in many ways, God spoke to our fathers by the prophets, but in these last days He has spoken to us by His Son, whom He appointed the heir of all things, through whom also He created the world. He is the radiance of the glory of God and the exact imprint of His nature, and He upholds the universe by the word of His power. After making purification for sins, He sat down at the right hand of the Majesty on high (Hebrews 1:1–3).

Even Jesus looked to a Who other than Himself. Hebrews reveals Jesus has a high view of His Father. Apart from God, He could do nothing on His own. He would only be about His Father's business. When His disciples asked to see His Father, Jesus said when you look at Me, you see the Father. The Father and Son are one.

You become whomever you behold. "What comes into our minds when we think about God is the most important thing about us," writes A. W. Tozer in his book *Knowledge of the Holy*. The one you spend the most time with is the one you start to become like. The first step toward finishing your race is setting your gaze on Jesus. Stop looking to humanity. Jesus had twelve close friends and one betrayed Him. Your friends will let you down. Leaders you elevate will fall short of your unrealistic expectations. Parents and children will break your heart. None will be enough. Jesus is greater. He is your best example for how to finish.

When you focus on the life of Jesus, you'll discover His purpose. Luke 19:10 reveals Jesus came to this world to seek and save the lost. Jesus started His ministry by revealing His life's purpose. He continued to worship at the same synagogue in Nazareth He worshiped at as a child. When He stood up to teach, He opened the scroll to Isaiah and read a Messianic prophecy written 800 years earlier. Luke 4:18 relays the five purposes of Jesus: "The Spirit of the Lord is upon me, because he has anointed me to proclaim good news to the poor. He has sent me to proclaim liberty to the captives and recovering of sight to the blind, to set at liberty those who are oppressed."

Never was this more demonstrated than when Jesus encountered a bunch of religious folks who confronted a woman caught in the act of adultery. The law said she must die. Jesus took a knee and wrote something in the ground with His finger. The last time the finger of God wrote something was on Mount Sinai when He composed the ten commandments. This time, instead of giving the law, the finger of God was extending grace, mercy, and love. One by one her accusers dropped their rocks and left. Imagine the intimate moment between her and Jesus when He told her she would not be accused that day. But then He said, "Go and sin no more." Jesus is full of grace and truth. Grace says I love you no matter what. Truth says I must be honest with you no matter what.

You are never the same after a real encounter with Jesus. The starting line of your spiritual race begins when you place your trust in Jesus, the Son of God whom the Father raised from the dead. You too are a child of God. Your life has purpose. When you discover His purpose, you'll discover your purpose. "Truly, truly, I say to you, whoever believes in me will also do the works that I do; and greater works than these will he do, because I am going to the Father" (John 14:12). Sustaining a long-term race requires a growing faith and trust in Jesus. The spirit of Christ is in you to start and finish great works. As a follower of Jesus, you'll discover a race full of adventure and true life when you start fulfilling His purposes. You are created to run, not to stumble. Your race continues when you are being conformed to His character and image. By being obsessed and consumed with Jesus, your heart and mind will be occupied with thoughts that won't abandon you in your most difficult moments. In Him alone is the faith needed to run your race with endurance to the finish line. You are not meant to run your race alone; you are meant to finish it. And finish it well through a relationship with Jesus. He declared, "I will never leave you." He will always give you help when you need it most. Over and over, you will be tempted to quit. Your only shot at crossing your finish line is keeping your eyes, heart, and mind centered on Jesus.

"You are of God, little children, and have overcome them, because He who is in you is greater than he who is in the world" (1 John 4:4). Dig deep. You are stronger than you think you are because the spirit of Christ is in you. When you feel alone and hope seems too distant, know it would be unfortunate for you to give up now. Jesus never gave up on you! He will give you the strength and grace to continue. Know Him. Love Him. This is eternal life.[1] The only way to look past your struggle is to look upon Jesus. You've been searching for Him all along. Jesus will help you finish your race.

2

DIE DAILY

ABEL

Jesus is Lord of all or not at all.

"WELL . . . IT'S PRETTY OBVIOUS YOU ARE NOT AN ATHLETE," my physical therapist muttered.

"What do you mean? I play golf once a week for crying out loud," I shot back.

She gave me a look. "Riding around in your little golf cart will not get you in shape. You'll never change until you realize what your poor health is costing you."

I sat in her office because I blew out my knee playing dodge ball, but that was not the real problem. I had high cholesterol and was well north of 200 pounds. I was a poor model of physical health to my family and unfit to fulfill God's Kingdom purpose for my life. This hard conversation was the reality check I needed to put the golf sticks in the attic and buy a bike.

Are you ready to pay the price for what matters most? You must be willing to sacrifice your best if you desire the best results. The problem for most is the cost is too high.

It's no surprise that the author of Hebrews 12 starts the chapter with the word "therefore." Whenever you see that word, ask yourself why it's there. What follows in this chapter won't make sense unless you understand the significance of the "Endurance Runner Hall of Fame" listed in Hebrews 11. Abel is not mentioned first because he got a blue ribbon for coming out of the womb first. He is mentioned first because of what is recorded of him in Genesis 4. It reveals where the race of faith starts for us all.

"By faith Abel offered to God a more acceptable sacrifice than Cain, through which he was commended as righteous, God commending him by accepting his gifts. And through his faith, though he died, he still speaks" (Hebrews 11:4).

In Abel, we find someone who paid the ultimate price. The Lord was pleased with Abel's sacrifice because he gave the firstborn of his flock, but Cain's sacrifice of day-old fruit cost him nothing. He hung his head in shame because he didn't give what God desired. The way of Cain is the way of self-reliance, pride, self-will, and disobedience. By offering his leftovers, Cain joined others who would honor God by bringing what seemed right while their hearts were far from Him. Paying with a tip instead of the true cost will never meet God's standard.

Unlike his brother Cain, Abel sacrificed his very best. Abel's short life declares a pivotal message. Though he suffered a gruesome death at the hands of a jealous brother, his voice has lasted beyond the grave and his worship is forever recorded in the pages of sacred history. Abraham listened to Abel's voice when he gave God his very best: He obeyed God's command to tithe the first fruits of his produce. Hannah listened too when she gave God her firstborn son. God gave His very best. He offered Jesus, His only begotten Son. The sacrifice Jesus made was greater than Abel's. Jesus willingly gave up His life. Cain took Abel's life, but no one took Jesus' life from Him. Instead, Jesus was led to His death like a lamb to slaughter. He gave His very best when He paid the highest price of all. Hebrews says Jesus was the mediator of a new covenant. His blood spoke a "better word" than the blood of Abel. Hebrews 9:22 says, "without the shedding of blood there is no forgiveness of sins." Jesus was stripped of all dignity and hung naked on a cross. That cross means love. Jesus unselfishly chose the highest good of His Father for you. That is what love does. Matthew 26:28 says, "For this is my blood of the covenant, which is poured out for many for the forgiveness of sins."

In the example of Abel, we see the starting line of the race: The moment the mind is awakened to the reality of our hopeless condition and the soul makes a sweet surrender to God. We must pass through death to truly live.

Unlike Cain, I'm grateful God spared my life when I only gave leftovers. Soon after starting Gateway Fellowship Church, I was tempted to quit. Attendance and offerings were in sharp decline, and I quickly ran out of savings to pay for even the simplest repairs in our humble, rented house. But my troubles didn't end with financial worries. My friends who surrendered their lives to Jesus no longer showed up in the teacher's lounge at Bob J. Beard Elementary School to receive the vital follow-up they needed to fill in their blanks. Then, worst of all, the school district called me in to give me official notification that we could no longer worship at the school.

Our church family was homeless.

The afternoon I submitted my resume to Gold's Gym and my wife's application to Starbucks, I drove to the small town of Leakey, nestled in the Texas "Hill Country." The first day of my week of solitude at the same H-E-B camp I attended as a high schooler was a full-blown pity party. I sulked, kicked rocks, and questioned everything. I was a failure who sucked at life. I had zero motivation to continue. I awoke the next morning and hiked to a familiar hillside by a river. There, the Holy Spirit led me to the very same oak tree where God called me to the ministry seventeen years before. The sick feeling in the pit of my stomach gave way to tears. God broke me. He convicted me of placing my health, marriage, and ministry before Him and showed me I had a serious pride problem. I felt my way was best. But God would not allow me to rob Him of His glory. I had based the vision for Gateway Fellowship Church on my own abilities, so God let me fail. He let me fail so I could acknowledge I couldn't do it without Him. Kneeling there beneath those branches, broken and weeping, I repented for my pride, mourned my sin, and died to my own dreams. That old tree became my rugged cross.

The forgiveness I received that morning was liberating. The Holy Spirit birthed a deep hunger and desire to start over. I hiked down from the oak grove to the headwaters of the Frio River. During my stay seventeen years before, it was tradition for all the high school guys to make their way to the ledge along the side of the river and hurl themselves four feet to plunge into the freezing, deep part of the water known as the Blue Hole. I stripped down to my skivvies and cannonballed in with my best William

Wallace scream. I lost my breath but took a new one. I was alive again.

No longer content with knowing about God, I wanted to know Him personally. Intimacy is more valuable than information, and relationship is more important than religion. I was done being a professional minister who, if truth be told, didn't really know Jesus, let alone know Him well enough to help others know Him. A fire was lit inside to know Jesus. For the next six months, I only read the Gospel of John. I memorized passage after passage. I studied Jesus' "I am" statements, realizing His claims had a claim on me. I discovered, underlined, and meditated on eighty-one attributes of His character and nature. I was experiencing real life promised by Jesus in John 17:3: "And this is eternal life, that they know you, the only true God, and Jesus Christ whom you have sent."

What if your life could echo throughout all of eternity? What if it too could speak beyond the grave someday? It cannot happen without sacrifice. Sacrifice is giving your best, not your leftovers. Sacrifice is giving out of your need, not your abundance. God did His part in salvation by sending His son Jesus to save you from your sin. Will you do your part?

DIE DAILY

Others will say, "compete to be first," "live for yourself," "get yours," "do what feels good," "pad your 401k." Jesus says something different. There is no shortcut. Jesus invites you to come and pay a cost. The price is your life. He declares in Mark 8:34–35, "If anyone would come after me, let him deny himself and take up his cross and follow me. For whoever would save his life will lose it, but whoever loses his life for my sake and the gospel's will save it." The degree of death determines the degree of life.

The apostle Paul writes a similar message to the Church in Romans 12:1: "I appeal to you therefore, brothers, by the mercies of God, to present your bodies as a living sacrifice, holy and acceptable to God, which is your spiritual worship."

This process of mortification sounds fun right? It can't be watered down, and there is no other way. Sin is serious. Sin is missing the mark. It is breaking God's law, and it is a departure from His character. Sin causes a gap in your intimacy with God. There is nothing you can do on your own to earn salvation. God has brought all things near through the blood of the cross. Every time you look at that cross, remember God did everything on His part to save you from your sin, your selfishness, and hell.

Jesus compares your race to a way that is narrow and difficult and found by only a few. It is difficult because dying to yourself is counter to the desires of your flesh and the culture of this world. There is a reality check waiting to happen so you too can discover you are nothing without Christ. When was the last time you were broken over your sinful condition in the presence of God? Only when you realize your sin broke His heart will you be comforted. Jesus said, "Blessed are the poor in spirit for theirs is the Kingdom of Heaven." Those who are rich in spirit have no need for a savior. Denying yourself and taking up your cross means being stripped of your pride. It means being broken, dependent, and humble. Find the tree that will be your rugged cross and give God space to do this work in you.

REPENT AND BELIEVE

Is there any part of your life not consistent with His character and teaching? If so, you are at war with God. Lordship equals obedience. As you obey what the Lord commands, you grow and develop. Your learning is progressive in the faith and knowledge of Jesus Christ. To be a disciple of Jesus is to be a learner. It never stops. You either obey or you don't. There is no middle ground. If I told you I'm 90 percent faithful to my wife, Stephanie, you wouldn't believe I'm faithful. When God looks at the condition of your heart, what does He see? Are you trusting and obeying or disobeying? If you are disobedient, His first request is that you repent. Stop sinning. God never gives a commandment without also giving the grace to obey it. When God asks for repentance, He means it. It's not pick and choose.

Repentance is a hard word, and, unfortunately, it is becoming extinct. But its process is vital to starting your race. It comes from the Greek word *metanoia*. "*Meta*" means change. "*Noia*" means mind. It literally means to change your mind. Change the way you think about God and yourself. Think like Jesus. Possess the mind of a Christian endurance runner. Ephesians 4:22–24 explains repentance this way: "to put off your old self, which belongs to your former manner of life and is corrupt through deceitful desires, and to be renewed in the spirit of your minds, and to put on the new self, created after the likeness of God in true righteousness and holiness." Repenting is the process of changing the way you think, talk, and act. You see Jesus as more valuable than the temptation of sin.

You are guilty and must take responsibility for your sin. It is essential to believe and trust in Jesus. However, salvation is more than raising a hand, saying a prayer, or walking up the aisle.

There is nothing wrong with that because it can be a very wonderful beginning. But it is the start of your race, not the finish line.

Acts 2:37–38 declares, "Now when they heard this they were cut to the heart, and said to Peter and the rest of the apostles, 'Brothers, what shall we do?' And Peter said to them, 'Repent and be baptized every one of you in the name of Jesus Christ for the forgiveness of your sins, and you will receive the gift of the Holy Spirit.'"

Dietrich Bonhoeffer refers to "cheap grace" as "the preaching of forgiveness without requiring repentance, baptism without church discipline. Communion without confession. Cheap grace is grace without discipleship, grace without the cross, grace without Jesus Christ."[1]

BLUE HOLE BAPTISM

The author of Hebrews 10:22 says, "Let us draw near with a true heart in full assurance of faith, with our hearts sprinkled clean from an evil conscience and our bodies washed with pure water." Find your Blue Hole in a river somewhere and get baptized. Jesus commanded you to be baptized in water because He never wants you to forget outwardly what you've expressed inwardly. It's both a wedding and a funeral. You now identify with Christ as His bride. Water baptism is your opportunity to celebrate and proclaim to all your friends that you are a new creation.

HONOR JESUS AS LORD

You'll never start your race well if it's all about you. Jesus asks a paralyzing question in Luke 6:46: "Why do you call me

'Lord, Lord,' and not do what I tell you?" Everyone wants a savior. No one wants a Lord. Christ is called Savior thirty-seven times. He is called Lord 7,836 times. It is healthy to bow. David writes in Psalm 24:1,"The earth is the Lord's and the fullness thereof, the world and those who dwell therein." There must be a bowing in reverence and fear before the holiness of the Lord God Almighty. God is God, and you are not. You don't make Jesus Lord. He is Lord on His own merit. It will never be about you. Your life revolves around the Lord Jesus. There is a link between salvation and lordship: You can't have one without the other. Glorify the King whose rightful place is on the throne of your heart.

You experience freedom when you realize you own nothing. You are entrusted with the air you breathe. Like Abel, acknowledge the principle of the first sacrifice. Abel gave the first of his flock. If God blesses you with children, dedicate them to Him. Acknowledge it all belongs to the Lord and be a good steward for Him.

God gave you time, treasure, and talents. Manage them well. What would it look like if you changed your thinking and believed the first part of the day belonged to the Lord? Imagine waking up and acknowledging Jesus as Lord and surrendering your day to Him. Would you spend time with the Lord through prayer and Scripture reading? Would you seek His Kingdom first? It takes faith to recognize God is first. Are you giving Him your best or what's left over?

If you live in the United States, you are blessed. Most of the world lives on less than two dollars a day. The Bible instructs you to give His tithe back to Him before anything else. It is sacred. Your entire paycheck is a gift from God, but He only asks for 10 percent to be given back to Him. There is more blessing on God's 90 percent than on your own 100 percent without Him.

My dad is the hardest working man I know. I watched him work full-time as a minister and as he also routinely worked extra jobs to provide for me and my two siblings. Even when finances were tight, he never robbed God. When I made collections during my first job as a paperboy in the fifth grade, my dad gave me three envelopes. The first was for God's tithe. The second was for savings. The third envelope was for spending. I'm grateful he didn't just teach me this at a young age. He also modeled it. When the time came to start a church and build a permanent home, it wasn't difficult for me to empty the savings account. Why? It all belonged to the Lord. His blessings far surpassed my sacrifices.

God has given you talents. It's not for your personal benefit alone. You are unique with strengths and gifts no one else has. How are you glorifying God with what He has entrusted you with? Build His Kingdom inside and outside the walls with those talents. Needs go unmet if you don't steward your gifts well.

SURRENDER YOUR RIGHTS

It will be tempting to cling tightly to what you feel is important. The reason we must endure death is because we will be tempted to earn God's salvation or favor. Your best performance apart from God is moldering laundry. He knows your heart and knows what you achieve out of pride and self-love. John the Baptist said, "He must increase. I must decrease." You surrender out of love, not out of labor.

What is the one thing God is telling you to do? Is there anything in your life that competes with Christ for your allegiance? Obey the one thing God is asking you to surrender. Giving up your rights is not burdensome; it's one of the most loving things you can do. Safety and security. Right to be offended. Losing self-control. Provision. Comfort. Achievement. Did Jesus hold on to these rights? Does Jesus want this for you? He says if you don't take up your cross and follow Him, you can't be His disciple. What is the cross? It's not jewelry or wall art, its death. It's an invitation to come and die.

Give up the right to have your own way. Jesus has a demand on your life. You have been "bought with a price." You must set aside your preferences. The litmus test of "dying daily" is asking those closest to you if you demonstrate more fruit of the Spirit than you used to. Are you more patient than you were six months ago? Do you have more self-control with your words and thoughts than before? If not, it's time to take up your cross again.

Running your race means not leaning on your own understanding or relying on your own human efforts. It means being dead to your sin. Imagine what life could be if you didn't care about getting credit for your accomplishments? No ego. No pride. Train yourself to see your life with the eternal prize always in mind.

Surrender to God your very best. God the Father gave you His best in the form of His only begotten son Jesus. Jesus gave you His best in the form of His life. Don't dare insult those gifts with leftovers. If God gave His best for you, give Him your best in return. You must be ready to sacrifice anything for the glory of God. Then, and only then, will your life "echo throughout eternity."

3

WALK WITH GOD

ENOCH

A soul cannot seek close fellowship with God...without a very honest and entire surrender to all His will.

ANDREW MURRAY

ONLY A FEW WEEKS AFTER COMPLETING PHYSICAL THERAPY for my dislocated knee and torn tendons, I prepared to toe the line for my first Olympic distance triathlon called the Arkan-Thaw Triathlon. Located about twenty miles southeast of Little Rock, Arkansas, the triathlon required each athlete to swim one mile through the shallow waters of Lake Norrell, ride a bike for a hilly, challenging twenty-five miles, and then somehow find the strength to run six miles over a course littered with extremely steep hills.

It was early April and the brisk, morning air set my teeth on edge and my nerves buzzing. Would I finish in victory or defeat? The race ahead was daunting because of my short training time, the untested and imposing difficulty of the course, and, if I can be vulnerable here, I'd shown up without even the ghost of a plan. Was it reckless? Probably. But, I couldn't back down and surrender to the fear of failure. I had to at least try. So, I pushed all the reasons why I should quit out of my head and set my mind on the finish line. Despite my questionable health and poor chances, I would give it all I had. Then, just five minutes before the start, I noticed a table full of food. I gorged on nutritional bars, strawberries, and bananas until I was completely full. It may have been a risk to eat so soon before racing, but there was no way I was going to run out of gas.

At the sharp blast of the whistle, adrenaline coursed through my veins. I sprinted and then dove into the freezing water. Fifty yards in, I was in the leading pack and doing well before the inevitable happened. Panic set in when I was suddenly engulfed in what can only be described as a washing machine of choppy waves swarming with churning bodies. Elbows from all sides pounded into me like sharp rocks and quickly knocked my goggles off, restricting my sight. I kept swimming hard, but, unbeknownst to me, I was headed in the wrong direction and into the wide center of the lake.

Minutes stretched into what felt like an hour or more. Why hadn't I reached the shore? Surely, I had swum a mile by now. Despair, doubt, and crippling fear shot through me as time dragged on with no end in sight. What felt like lead weights strapped to me grew heavier by the second. Every stroke of my arms and kick of my feet felt like a battle for my life. My mind boiled down until all logic and clarity evaporated. When would it end?

Energy depleted, heart racing, breath gone, and without hope, I prepared to drown.

Then, incredibly, a new wave of strength came, my thoughts cleared, and logic overcame the fear as deeper survival instincts kicked in. I stopped thrashing through the water, rolled over, and floated on my back, taking deep, long breaths for several minutes. Brain and body reset by much-needed oxygen, I looked around as I treaded water, regained my bearings, and realized I had swum 300 yards off course. Discouraged but renewed by the sight of the shore, I rolled back over, dug deeper, and began again.

It was no small miracle that I reached the shore, dragged myself onto my bike, clipped my cleats into the matching teeth on the pedals, and took off down the pavement. I knew cycling was my strength, so I pushed hard to catch up.

Then, out of nowhere, a few miles in, I encountered excruciating stomach pains.

I was cramping due to my high pace and the copious amount of food I ignorantly consumed moments before the race. My insides turned inside out as everything came back up in a violent display in the prickly weeds alongside the road.

For the second time in two hours, I felt like I would see Jesus. The pain never went away, but I refused to give in. Incredibly, God gave me the strength to overcome the pain, and I ended up finishing the cycling portion with most of my fellow racers. Physically spent, I ignored temptation and refused to eat or drink anything else. Halfway through my run, severe pain hit like a beating hammer to the head and fatigue sucked away almost everything I had left. I can say without a doubt that this time the miracle wasn't a small one when I limped in, representing last place, holding my side, and stumbling straight to the field ambulance. Nothing was seriously wrong with me, only my pride.

I learned a valuable lesson that day. You can't wing an endurance event. A strict training plan is essential to finishing well. "Let us run with endurance the race that is set before us."[1] It's what you do in private leading up to the endurance event that determines how you finish. It will hold you accountable for exercising multiple days a week, increasing time and distance every week until the week of tapering and resting before the race. A good plan will encourage you to practice your nutrition during your training runs, so you can manage the essential fuel needed for a long day on the course. Most endurance athletes need to consume 300 calories per hour to finish. Your body needs to consistently refuel what it expends. If it cannot, it will begin to eat itself because it was not properly prepared.

Just as God created your body, He created your soul. There is a running parallel of principles you can apply to both. Your spiritual race will be won or lost during training. It will be tempting to ignore spiritual disciplines needed for a healthy relationship with the Lord, but it becomes your foundation. You are as close to God as you want to be. You must take responsibility for your spiritual life with the same diligence you need for running a long-distance race. The process God uses to build your faith is much like endurance training. Growth and a close relationship with God only come through training. A. W. Tozer says, "In the Bible, the race of life is never considered from the viewpoint of speed. We're to run it with patience. It takes time and discipline. Finishing isn't the end goal, it's finishing well, fighting the good fight and keeping the faith."[2]

Enoch is the next endurance runner introduced by the Hebrews writer. He was listed because Enoch exemplifies an essential quality.

> By faith Enoch was taken away so that he did not see death, "and was not found, because God had taken him"; for before he was taken he had this testimony, that he pleased God. But without faith it is impossible to please Him, for he who comes to God must believe that He is, and that He is a rewarder of those who diligently seek Him (Hebrews 11:5–6, NKJV).

Enoch is intriguing because he never tasted death on Earth. I imagine God liking his boy Enoch so much that He couldn't wait for him to die and just took him up. What was unique about Enoch? Scripture reveals he *pleased God*. Why? Because day after day and year after year, Enoch diligently sought the Lord. Enoch showed great care in his pursuit of fellowship with his Lord. Making his righteousness even more incredible, Enoch lived during the horrifying times before the flood when men and women poisoned the Earth, destroyed each other, and had only evil in their hearts. It was an age filled with violence and conditions unlike anything you could imagine. It could not have been easy or simple to follow the Lord during that time. But Enoch walked with God despite his surroundings and circumstances because he was committed to a life of faith manifested in communion with God.

Every follower of Jesus must learn to walk with the Lord. Stop being dependent on anyone else but Jesus. In James 4:8, His Word promises that when we draw near to God, He draws near to us. Jesus told us what it looked like to walk with God when He said, "Abide in Me, and I in you. As the branch cannot bear fruit by itself, unless it abides in the vine, neither can you, unless you abide in Me."[3] Jesus repeats the word "abide" ten times in

John 15. It means a life-giving connection. If you could see inside a vine, you wouldn't notice where the vine ended and the branches began. This imagery describes your union with Christ. Intimacy with the Lord must be your highest priority. Nothing can take its place. God will not force you to walk with Him, but He will convict you of its importance and the laziness and lack of planning that led you further from Him.

The author of Hebrews writes, "About this we have much to say, and it is hard to explain, since you have become dull of hearing. For though by this time you ought to be teachers, you need someone to teach you again the basic principles of the oracles of God. You need milk, not solid food, for everyone who lives on milk is unskilled in the word of righteousness, since he is a child. But solid food is for the mature, for those who have their powers of discernment trained by constant practice to distinguish good from evil" (Hebrews 5:11–14).

The author is taking a bunch of whiny believers behind the woodshed. They needed a wake-up call. There is nothing wrong with a four-month-old being fed in his high chair, but you would want to throat punch a forty-year-old man if he was still sitting in that same high chair demanding baby carrots from his mom. Will milk alone satisfy the nutritional needs of an adult?

Put down the bottle. Get out of the high chair. Take that stained bib off. When you dig into the Bible, you will find a feast beyond your wildest imagination waiting for you in the higher truths found in God's Word. No amount of busyness, religious books, sermons, or podcasts can replace it. All of these things are good, but they're like condiments—meant to go along with the real food, not take its place. Make no mistake, there is no substitute on this Earth for the "Living Bread"[4] found only in the Word.

RELATIONSHIP OVER RELIGION

Genesis says Enoch walked faithfully with God.[5] The imagery of the two walking together is one of unity. Amos 3:3 asks the following question: "Can two walk together, except they be agreed?" But what does that look like?[6] I believe Enoch was listed before Noah not only for chronological reasons as a forefather of Noah but also because Enoch understood the heart of service manifests as an overflow from a passionate relationship with God. Your relationship with God will always matter more to Him than what you do. Jesus didn't just come to empower you. He also came to reconcile you to Himself, to restore the relationship we were created for. Jesus said in John 17 that He desired us to be with Him, to be one with Him as He and the Father are one.[7] Through a healthy relationship with God, your spiritual walk will be a journey of growth and service. To "walk with God" communicates relationship.

My family and I are blessed to live several miles north of the beautiful city of San Antonio in a neighborhood tucked away in the evergreen-blanketed, rolling hills of central Texas. Known by locals as the "Hill Country," the area is unique. Few other places offer the serenity of a stroll through a forest touched by the wildness of Texas where you'll find oak groves, cedar trees, tall and yellow wild rye, switch grass, and the occasional prickly cactus. Often my wife and I will leave the comfort of our home and take walks together through the wild woods near our home after work. We don't talk ministry and sometimes we don't talk at all. We're spending time together. We're pursuing each other, abandoning the pressures of life to grow deeper in our unity.

People used by God for great purposes prioritized spiritual disciplines behind the scenes when no one was watching. They read the Word, prayed, studied, pursued, memorized Scripture, and worshipped their God in quiet intimacy away from it all. Their ministry flowed out of their walk with God.

The single greatest book that helped my walk with the Lord is *The Practice of the Presence of God*, written by a seventeenth-century monk and humble kitchen worker named Brother Lawrence. No matter where he was or what he was doing, he was acutely aware of the presence of God. Brother Lawrence said, "In order to form a habit of conversing with God continually, and referring all we do to Him; we must at first apply to Him with some diligence: but that after a little care we should find His love inwardly excites us to it without any difficulty."[8]

TRAINING PLAN

Are you pleasing the Lord with the time you spend with Him? He longs to take a walk with you. It's during this time He shapes your character and deepens your spiritual roots. Ask the Holy Spirit to lead you to the right training plan. None are perfect. No one has the best model. What works for one will not work for another. The most important principle is quality time with the Lord. A strong devotional life is rooted in a personal relationship with Jesus. It is crucial to finishing your spiritual race with "all endurance."[9] Discipleship is about listening and obeying. But how can you obey if you don't take the time to listen? Seek God for the personal path He's created just for you and Him, your very own walk through the woods.

So much gets in the way in our busy modern lives. Time is sucked away by the constant bombardment of communication and information, the day-to-day demands of longer workdays, less vacation time, and the demand to perform. Step out of your comfort zone, break your routine, and take the time to find a training plan. You may try many that simply don't work for you. Don't give up. When you hear from God, obey and follow the training plan He's leading you to. Following it will keep you consistent and on course, and it will ultimately lead you to spiritual maturity. The Lord rewards those who diligently seek Him. "Then you will call upon me and come and pray to me, and I will hear you. You will seek me and find me, when you seek me with all your heart."[10] Missionary Dick Brogden says, "Discipline leads to desire, and desire leads to delight."

DESIRE

If you love Jesus, you will naturally want to spend time with Him. Your training plan starts in your heart. Unless your desire to walk with the Lord is more than anything else, it won't last for long. What if the desire to spend time with the Lord was equal to the need to breathe? Jesus says blessed are those who hunger and thirst for righteousness for they will be filled.[11]

Desire to take a walk with Him more than anyone else. You can't value the voice of a pastor or a friend more than the voice of Jesus. There will be times when you don't feel like it, but you can't be led by your emotions. No one who begins a run continuously likes it. The pounding of the pavement creates pain in places you didn't know you had. But if you stick with it, you'll soon experience a "runner's high"!

The desire for a deeper relationship with the Lord spurred me and my friend Kyle Volkmer to take a trip to the Middle East. We didn't just want a deeper relationship with the Lord, we wanted to be better husbands, fathers, and pastors. When we pursue God, we don't just grow closer to Him. We also find that everything else in our lives that was out of alignment—every strained relationship, hurt, and misunderstanding—gradually transforms into closer unity with others.

One specific desire we had was to study the character and nature of Jesus as the Good Shepherd. This led us to the Wadi Rum Desert in the country of Jordan. We arrived at midnight, and when we awoke our breath was taken from us because of the desert's sheer beauty. It was like being on the set of the movie *Indiana Jones and the Last Crusade* with 400-foot rocky cliffs that seemed to be rusting with age.

We spent a couple of days with a seventy-year-old shepherd named Nassar. This older man had weathered skin and layers of clothing. A typical day for him began with an early morning inspection of his flock. Nassar would take every lamb into his arms and carefully observe their eyes and general health before physically bringing them to their mothers.

That morning, after inspecting a small lamb, Nassar placed one in my arms and pointed to a sheep that must have been its mother because she gave me a long, suspicious look. Carefully carrying the soft lamb, I walked over to its mother, lifted her hind leg aside, and gently laid the lamb down next to her, making sure the lamb latched on. The Holy Spirit struck me with an epiphany as the lamb drank the milk. He brought this Scripture to mind: "Like newborn infants, long for the pure spiritual milk, that by it you may grow up into salvation."[12]

You may be in a wilderness like that little lamb, but the Good Shepherd hasn't left your side for a moment. He's provided you with the spiritual nutrients you need just as that mother sheep provided for her lamb. God's spiritual milk is found in His Word. But not just in Scripture. It is also in your pursuit of Jesus. Jesus is the Word! He told the Samaritan woman at the well, "whoever drinks of the water that I will give him will never be thirsty again. The water that I will give him will become in him a spring of water welling up to eternal life."[13] Ask the Lord to give you a craving for Scripture because only He can provide the true food, His Word.[14]

FIND YOUR SECRET PLACE

No human showed more devotion to His Father than Jesus. He understood the importance of getting away to a secret place: "And rising very early in the morning, while it was still dark, He departed and went out to a desolate place, and there He prayed."[15] He said to His followers, "But when you pray, go into your room and shut the door and pray to your Father who is in secret. And your Father who sees in secret will reward you."[16] Find your secret place and protect it. It may be a closet, hunting blind, porch, or even a trail in the woods. Go there often, not just when you feel like it. Make going there a discipline.

Seeking my wife is not a check mark on a list. I want to be with her every day. I made a commitment to her. And the more time I spend pursuing her, the more in love I become. Seek God in your hiding place. Don't just talk, listen. Be still and know that He is God and you are not.[17] You will be amazed at what the Lord shares with you every day! Whether it's revelation, vision, or simply the solace and sweet comfort of His presence.

BIBLE STUDY

I grew up in church but struggled with living out a consistent, personal study of the Bible. While attending a church planting conference in Orlando, God gave me a light-bulb moment. As I listened to Pastor Wayne Cordero share his story about how he grew deeper through Bible study, the Lord had me lean in and listen. Through his testimony and example, Wayne introduced me to the acrostic S.O.A.P., which can be applied to any passage in Scripture.[18]

- Scripture: Meditate on one verse in a chapter you read
- Observation: Write down the lesson revealed
- Application: List ways you can implement the lesson in your own personal life
- Prayer: Thank God for understanding truth and ask Him to help you apply it

Don't just open the Bible at random places. Be diligent and read through an entire book at a time. This acrostic has transformed my life. I pray it does the same for you!

MEMORIZE

I have found great value in memorizing Scripture, and you can too. The Word says to hide His Word in your heart, to meditate on it day and night. He promises not a single one of His words will come back void.[19] Memorizing the Word will bring increase in your life in ways you couldn't even imagine.[20] While on a mission trip to the Dream Center in Los Angeles, I met a homeless man named Thomas. He was facing the exterior of an old hospital with his head bowed. The old, worn-out jacket he was wearing made it easy to guess he didn't have much. Thomas was focused on a key ring filled with white index cards. Each card had one Scripture verse written on it by hand.

With infectious enthusiasm, Thomas explained to me how memorizing and quoting Scripture helped him overcome issues that had imprisoned him and controlled his life. He found freedom in Christ through His Word![21] The Holy Spirit quickly reminded me of Jesus hiding God's Word in His heart and using it as a defense against temptation when attacked by the devil.[22]

After returning home from the conference, Thomas's bold example remained in the forefront of my mind. I sat down, gathered some index cards, and kept them with my devotional journal. As I spent daily time with the Word, I wrote down key verses and wound them onto a large key ring. Sooner than I thought, my key ring began to fill. Whenever I needed an encouraging word from the Lord, one He had personally given to me as a life verse, I would pour over those index cards and be reminded of God's faithfulness.

How can you be creative in memorizing Scripture? Perhaps you learn by listening. Listen to one of the many free recordings of Scripture, write down the verse the Holy Spirit highlighted for you, and pray for the Lord to write it on your heart.[23] Whatever works for you, get serious about memorizing Scripture, and the Holy Spirit will use His spiritual milk to help you grow, pray, witness, and resist temptation.[24]

Your Lord Jesus desires to spend intimate time with you. The longer your race, the more tempting it is to believe the lie that Jesus becomes the means to an end. Your heart will harden if you go through the motions: "I know you are enduring patiently and bearing up for my name's sake, and you have not grown weary. But I have this against you, that you have abandoned the love you had at first. Remember therefore from where you have fallen; repent, and do the works you did at first."[25] It's important to spend time with Him so your heart stays tender. Never forget, Jesus is the author and finisher. Reject your fleshly desires, lean in, and listen carefully to the words of Jesus.[26] If you want to walk with God, you must walk in complete surrender.

4

SWING THAT HAMMER

NOAH

What God does in you, He does through you.

LIKE "SUGAR-PLUMS" THAT "DANCED IN THEIR HEADS," A BELT buckle danced in my head for three long years. It was a big, flashy, southern one, like the ones I grew up seeing in Texas. But this particular belt buckle could only be earned on a bike in Leadville, Colorado. Listed as the highest city in the United States, Leadville sits at an elevation of 10,152 feet and is nestled in a valley situated between two mountain ranges of the Rockies. Beyond its ranking as the highest city in the United States, Leadville is arguably best known for its ultramarathon races. One of those races is the Leadville Trail 100 (LT100), a one-hundred-mile, mountain-bike race, promoted as "the race of all races." Even attracting the likes of Lance Armstrong for two years in a row, it is one of the best known, if not *the* best known, marathon events in all of mountain-bike racing. But this treacherous trail doesn't just wind up and down through mountains; it boasts an infamous uphill climb of over 3,000 feet to an elevation peaking at 12,424 feet.

For those of you who have never been at such a high altitude, let me tell you, it's a ruthless environment for physical exertion. The air is so thin that the lower air pressure makes it seem like there is less oxygen, causing what's known as altitude sickness. Your muscles and brain cannot function correctly at such a high altitude without proper, rigorous training. There are a dizzying number of dangerous outcomes for the unprepared.

It is a great feat just to finish. But crossing the finish line wouldn't give you the coveted belt unless you finished in under twelve hours. One hundred miles through the Rockies while feeling like you are sucking oxygen through a stir straw. Twelve hours.

Every time I look at my LT100 belt, I remember the pain and suffering. Not only on the day of the event but also throughout the three years of training leading up to it. The hard work included many lonely, hours-long rides on trails in the Texas Hill Country before daylight. I once rode over a rattlesnake and had a crash that flung my body over my handlebars on a downhill slope. Every training ride in the heat prepared me for the LT100.

Anyone who has finished a marathon remembers the long training runs a couple of weeks before race day. Essential training is necessary if you want to strap on that elusive belt buckle or feel the satisfying, heavy weight of a medal as it hangs around your neck at the finish line. The harder the race, the sweeter the prize. Every step or turn of the pedal during the last three miles feels like torture, but the pain subsides when the vision of the finish line appears in the distance. Faith gets you off the starting block, but perseverance, faithfulness, and long obedience will urge you past the finish line. In a generation where everyone gets a participation trophy, kids expect an instant reward without hard work. We have been conditioned by a quick-fix, fast-food, overnight, one-click culture. Entitlement and laziness are the hallmarks here, and they create a perfect contrast to a good work ethic and personal responsibility.

There may not be a more hard-working endurance runner than Noah. God rewards those who diligently seek Him, but He is also a judge to those who reject His commands in disobedience and sin. Noah lived in a wicked world, one we could hardly imagine. In those days, every single thought of mankind was continuously evil.[1] God saw something unique in Noah, so He gave him a vision.

"By faith Noah, being divinely warned of things not yet seen, moved with godly fear, prepared an ark for the saving of his household, by which he condemned the world and became heir of the righteousness which is according to faith" (Hebrews 11:7, NKJV).

OWN THE VISION

Noah received a daunting vision: one of the judgment to come. God showed him a massive 510-foot ark equal in length to one-and-a-half football fields. He told Noah to build it to exact specifications because He was sending a massive flood to destroy all people.[2] Though the vision was terrifying, a merciful God was saving a righteous generation through the preparation of a massive boat with primitive tools and supplies. Noah and his family would not perish. "Where there is no vision, the people perish."[3] This God-sized vision was far beyond Noah, and he knew it. He would need incredible faith to pick up that hammer. If he didn't, more lives would be lost, including those of his family.

What if every life is designed with a compelling vision to meet a desperate need? A God-sized vision and purpose are waiting to be fulfilled by you. Your purpose in life is at the intersection where your greatest passion meets a desperate need. How do you know it is your calling? You can't stop thinking about the idea whether you are in the shower or in bed. Trusted friends and Scripture confirm it. The Holy Spirit guides you with inner peace like a compass. All signs will point to it being right. E. Stanley Jones says, "It's unnatural for a Christian not to have an appetite for the impossible." Awaken to the great vision and commission Jesus gave you in Matthew 28:19: "Go therefore and make disciples of all the nations." And know this: There is another flood of judgment coming, but this time it will be a "great tribulation, such as has not been from the beginning of the world until now, no, and never will be."[4] The signs of Christ's return are happening all around us. There will be more earthquakes, more hurricanes, and more war. Sense the urgency of the Lord. The stakes have never been higher. You are called to be God's own method of saving a generation. To ignore this vision from Jesus is to amble aimlessly while people perish.

Don't listen to the voice saying you don't matter or think, "what could I possibly add?" The answer is you can add Jesus! You are His hands and feet to those who are perishing, a light in a darkening world. God has a vision for your life. Take hold of the Jeremiah 29:11 promise and never let go: "For I know the plans I have for you, declares the Lord, plans for welfare and not for evil, to give you a future and a hope." Ignore the haters and doubters, even the one inside your own mind. God has given you a burden and wired you in a special way with a unique calling. There are ways of fulfilling the Great Commission no one has tried before. Every leader who finishes strong ran their race aware of the vision of a great destiny. Decisions are based solely on vision. God has an eternal purpose for you to fulfill. His Kingdom is advancing and, incredibly, you're invited to play a role.

FEAR OF THE LORD

Often when we hear the phrase "fear God," we think of being scared, and rightly so. The Word says to not fear man but to "fear Him who can destroy both soul and body in Hell."[5] The fear of the Lord isn't so much being afraid of God as it is being terrified to live life separated from Him. But as children of God, we know our eternal resting place is with God.[6] This kind of fear should make you feel safe, as a child feels safe in his or her father's arms. God will protect you, and He is your Rock when the floodwaters rise.

Genesis records Noah as a righteous man.[7] Noah had to be fully convinced God would do what He said. He was moved to work out God's vision by a deep, sincere fear of the Lord, and that "fear" was a powerful drive. In his heart of hearts, Noah knew the rain and flood were coming as a righteous, holy judgment upon an evil generation. And he knew if he didn't trust God, he and his family would die like the rest of mankind: alienated and separated from God.

Building a large structure like the ark could not have gone unnoticed or without ridicule. Many people must have heard of the coming wrath, but only Noah heard *and* obeyed. Just as Noah lived out what he heard from God, we should hear and put into practice the vision God is calling us to follow because faith without works is dead.[8]

This reverential awe vital to living out a godly life seems missing in this generation, even more so than in the ones that came before it. Perhaps that is why over half of those in this generation who were raised in church drop out by adulthood. The waters rose, the storms came, and they found their houses fallen because they were built on the sand. They did not hear and obey.

My good friend Kyle Volkmer explains it like this: "Nothing is more desperately needed in this time and hour than to have a supernatural revelation of the fear of the Lord. The Church in the United States is generally blind, naked, miserable, and poor. This is undoubtedly due to the irreverence toward the holiness of God. The fear of the Lord is the beginning of knowledge, the precursor and foundation of our faith, a fountain of riches and life, and it is the everlasting Gospel."[9] Kyle can drop the mic. He's right and so is Solomon, the wisest man of another generation who proclaims, "The end of the matter; all has been heard. Fear God and keep his commandments, for this is the whole duty of man" (Ecclesiastes 12:13).

The secret of the Lord is with those who fear Him. Fear is the root leading to obedience. What God does in you, He does through you.

WORK HARD

Vision is the fun part. Everyone loves to dream. The challenge is the execution of the vision. It would be a long time before Noah ever felt the stormy wind begin to blow or saw the rain clouds gathering, but he believed and acted anyway. That is what faith does. Although the exact time it took Noah to build the ark is not specifically mentioned, historians believe it would have taken, at most, nearly sixty-five years to build.

I can't even imagine that. I get frustrated after forty-five minutes of building a Lego Resistance X-Wing Fighter with my son. Noah swung that hammer long before he took his cruise. Faith put a hammer in Noah's hand, and faithfulness drove the last nail into the boat years later.

There was another who picked up a hammer. His name was Jesus. As a carpenter, He faithfully swung that hammer for fifteen years before His Father sent Him out into public ministry. Imagine the development that needed to take place in the Son of God. He was sent to save the world. What a responsibility! So why "waste" so many years as a carpenter? It had to do with Jesus' heart. He wasn't concerned with "important," immediate ministry. He wasn't afraid of "missing" His calling. He wasn't worried about rushing God's timing. His only concern was to be about His Father's business.[10] And here we see the heart of Jesus. Humble. Submissive. Patient. Faithful. Hardworking Servant. Jesus said He came to serve and not to be served.[11] He took the humble nature of a servant who started as a carpenter and ended as a towel boy when he took a knee to wash the feet of His disciples. Nothing was beneath Him.

Being a simple carpenter in a small Jewish village may have seemed like a "little" vision, but you grow by finishing the little things and finishing them well. Faithfulness in small tasks prepares you for greater works. Jesus said in Luke 16:10, "One who is faithful in a very little is also faithful in much." A life of faith is a life lived in long, faithful obedience to God. Persevering obedience is hard work. Noah and Jesus teach you a valuable lesson when you look close and lean in. They reveal the clear distinction between vision and the hard work it takes to fulfill it.

While attending college, I interned under a great pastor named Scott Wilson. I told him that God called me to the ministry and that I would commit to serving and learning from him as my mentor. Scott agreed, but the ministry didn't end up looking the way I expected.

For two years, I never stepped foot on stage during service. Instead, I set up the stage and stacked chairs in a gym. I never once spoke into a mic, I never once publicly led a prayer. But I trusted God's development in me and that He would fulfill the vision He'd called me to. The strong work ethic Scott instilled in me by asking me to do "behind the scenes" ministry was just the right "hammer" to prepare me for the God-sized vision waiting to be realized in my life.

I graduated college with a ministry degree and a readiness to pursue the vision God birthed in me two years earlier. My first assignment was also not what I was expecting. I was hired to serve as a youth pastor in a small church in McKinney, Texas. I made $150 per week with my wife and me also doing the janitorial work. My hammer was a toilet brush. After serving there, we moved to Colorado and continued our bi-vocational ministry of youth pastor and janitor. We did it because it was the only way we could pay rent. But God had a higher purpose. He was developing character. If God could trust us with swinging whatever "hammer" He gave us, He could trust us with His greatest treasure: people.

When we started Gateway, I became lead pastor. But God kept the "hammer" of humility in my hands. For seven years—364 Sundays—we arrived at 6:50 a.m. to set up and tear down in a school, then in a hotel, and finally in a movie theater. But every morning began the same way. Get there two hours before service began—which was before sunrise during most of the year—open trailers, pull equipment out of aging wooden cases, set equipment up, and troubleshoot twisted and broken cables, missing stools, or mic stands. Once service began, I preached, dripping in sweat from swinging that hammer. Whenever volunteers would encourage me to sleep in, to let them set up so I could come in late, I couldn't say yes. Honestly, I didn't trust my heart. God wanted me to keep serving to keep me humble.

Paul writes to a church family in Corinth, "I'm sure you've been to the stadium at least once to see athletes race. Everyone runs; only one wins. Run to win. All good athletes train hard. They do it for a gold medal that tarnishes and fades, but you're after one that's eternal gold. I don't know about you, but I'm running hard for that finish line. I'm giving it everything I've got. No sloppy living for me! I'm staying alert and in top condition. I'm not going to tell everyone else all about the good news only to be caught napping and miss out on it myself."[12] I'm swinging that hammer and not putting it down until the vision is fulfilled.

But what if God gives you a hammer outside of your comfort zone? We weren't called out of darkness and into marvelous light to be comfortable.[13] We're called into war, into daily battles.[14] We're citizens of heaven living and working behind enemy lines.[15] I'm sure Noah felt foolish sometimes building a boat when there was no water, but in time God proved Himself faithful. It may seem ridiculous at the time, but you should never resent the hammer placed in your hands. God placed it there. It is just as vital to ministry as the vision.

Never be afraid of hard work. This is where God develops your character and tests you to see if He can trust you with a higher Kingdom purpose. To achieve something important, whatever work is required is also important, no matter what it looks like.

Cleaning a toilet or setting up a stage might not seem important or noteworthy to you, but the "important" ministry couldn't function properly without it. Sure, it's not always pretty or fun. The season between the vision fulfilled and the grunt work behind the scenes and out of the limelight can be long. But never quit early. Swinging that hammer will enable you to "fly" one day.

You may be tempted to scream, "I don't want to do this! It's not my spiritual strength. God, You gave me the vision, why aren't You fulfilling it?" Your spiritual gift is called denying yourself and taking up your cross. Hard training is the process by which God develops your character. He cares more about your foundation. This is when God does His greatest transformation in your life. Trust God's timing. Why do you do the things you do, and who do you do them for? Never forget your why behind all the hard work. Be faithful in the little. Love finds a need and meets it. There are no small roles in the Kingdom of God. What need isn't being met that you can meet right now?

God doesn't call the qualified, He qualifies the called. You must run without the credit, without the paycheck, without the recognition from the stage, and even without the title. You will not have the endurance to cross the finish line without the hard training.

SAVE SOULS

The rainbow became God's promise to man that He would never destroy the Earth with a flood again, but to Noah it was also a reminder of God rewarding him with the salvation of his family. God will do the same for you. There is another judgment coming. This one will be far worse, and it is coming soon for this world is "being kept until the day of judgment" for the "destruction of the ungodly."[16] You have a Kingdom purpose with an eternal prize. Imagine spending eternity with Jesus and those you helped reach. Will you obey the call to go and make disciples?

The great theologian Dietrich Bonheoffer once said, "One act of obedience is better than a hundred sermons." Why is that? When you obey, you are literally living out the Word of God. You are on His mission, and His mission will never fail.

I once acted in obedience, and it became greater than 300 sermons.

Gateway Fellowship Church began in our living room with eight people on a Labor Day weekend. The vision God gave us was to become friends with 1,200 people in our community. We hung butcher paper on our wall, wrote the names of our new friends, and prayed in response to the burden. Our mission was to help them become devoted followers of Jesus. We stopped going through the drive-through and paying at the pump and instead sought face-to-face interactions. We introduced ourselves to our neighbors and hung out in coffee shops. We went *to* the sick and hurting, even in bars, following our personal convictions without making anyone feel judged. That's what Jesus did, and that's what we knew He wanted us to do.

The echo of God's heart to mine is remembering that every number has a name, every name has a story, and every story matters to God.

Let me close this chapter with one story, one name I will never forget. I met Val after school while we waited to pick up our daughters. We discovered we lived in the same neighborhood and shared a passion for mountain biking. I got his number and we rode together the next day. A few weeks later, Val stopped riding because of a brain tumor. He declined my offer to pray together because he stopped believing there was a God.

I listened to his story over pecan waffles in the kitchen nook of his home. It was cloudy and the tension was real. Moments passed before we started talking about the elephant in the room. Val stood up to pour another cup of coffee and then looked out the window. I could sense the heaviness on his heart.

After a moment of thick silence, he said, "My dad abused my mom for years. He cheated on her too."

I didn't know what to say.

"I was just a kid—five, I think," he began and then paused with bitterness and pain just beneath the surface of his expression. "I prayed hard. I asked God over again to make my dad stop, to help my mom...but I guess He didn't care because it never stopped."

I told Val the same God he called out to when he was five was the same God who listened to him now. Another hard silence. I asked him if he was ready to surrender his life to Jesus. He said no thanks in a tone that sounded torn. It was obvious the Holy Spirit was drawing him close when he promised to call me if he changed his mind.

Two weeks later I went to visit Val in the hospital. While I was praying in the waiting room, my friend died of a brain seizure during his CT scan.

Devastated with grief, I left with an enormous hole in my heart and an unbearable weight of guilt for not doing more. I came home but couldn't talk to anyone. I rode my bike for hours and cried often. I had moved into this new community, and Val had become my closest friend, and he was taken away from me too soon.

The next day, his widow Debra showed up at my front door. Her eyes were swollen and her heart was heavier than mine. In her hands, she held a stack of journals—Val's journals. She said, "We don't belong to a church and don't know of another minister. Val would want you to officiate his funeral, but you have to read these first."

After Debra left, I retreated to my office, holding the journals tight to my chest. My friend was gone, but perhaps there was more to know about my friend in these pages. I began with the most recent entries, and I quickly discovered an entry from a few days before that described his spiritual journey like a ship returning to a harbor. What I read astounded me! Val made a confession to God! My friend was saved! As I read those sweet words, I couldn't help but weep with relief. Because of the saving grace of Jesus, I could be sorrowful over the death of my friend but rejoice over his eternal destination.

Before we ever had a worship service, we had a funeral. To know Val was to know his friends, his family, and his faith.

There in the chapel of the Sunset Funeral Home in San Antonio, Texas, I was surrounded by 350 of Val and Debra's friends and family. Stephanie and I had an incredible opportunity to share our story from the pulpit as people got up to honor Val. After hearing our story, Debra invited everyone to the grand opening of our church at Bob Beard Elementary School a few weeks later. Forty-one came, and eighteen of Val's friends and family surrendered their lives to Jesus at that first Sunday service on February 10, 2008. Many of them, including Debra and her daughter Isa, were baptized in water.

It was a bittersweet beginning for Gateway, but a beautiful example of how God brings death out of life. Just as He brought Noah and his family out of the flood, He brought Val out of death and into His arms. And He used Val's unique story to bring many others to salvation.

Souls matter to God. They must matter to you. Will you respond to God's unique plan for your life? Will you make a commitment to never stop swinging that hammer, even when the work gets hard? You never know what God will build through you. Even if it's just one soul reconciled to God, know that all of heaven rejoices in that moment!

5

BETTER TOGETHER

ABRAHAM and SARAH

If you want to go fast, go alone.
If you want to go far, go together.
AFRICAN PROVERB

SIDE BY SIDE AT THE STARTING LINE, STEPHANIE AND I LOOKED at each other and wondered what we had gotten ourselves into. It was a chilly fifty-eight degrees near Austin, Texas, and sunlight was just spilling over the horizon, illuminating the course stretching out before us. We were about to compete in the Muddy Buddy, an endurance race designed for partners. Stephanie and I would have to stay near each other and leapfrog through the course on foot and bike, through seven miles of obstacles and five separate challenges that ended in an infamous fifty-foot long mud pit.

And this race was supposed to be "fun."

At least, that's what our friends told us when they convinced us to sign up.

As soon as the gun blasted, we took off, leery of what lay ahead but a little hopeful it wouldn't be as bad as it looked from the starting line. After a couple of hours, we still hadn't finished. Stephanie and I endured pain, a flat tire, and a lot of mud everywhere—and I mean everywhere. But we were in this together, and the only way we'd finish would be side by side.

Marriage, like the Muddy Buddy, is a challenging endurance race designed for two. Taking off from that wedding-day starting line means problem-solving when things inevitably go wrong and getting banged up, bruised, dirty, wiped out, and discouraged when obstacle after obstacle arises. But you can't do it alone. Your race will be messy and sometimes seem impossible to complete, but it will always be better when you run it together.

While studying the endurance runners listed in Hebrews 11, I was intrigued to discover Abraham and Sarah are the only couple mentioned. Side by side and by faith, they accomplished a lot probably because they were "muddy buddies."

By faith Abraham obeyed when he was called to go out to a place he was to receive as an inheritance. He went out not knowing where he was going. By faith he went to live in the land of promise as he would in a foreign land, living in tents with Isaac and Jacob, heirs of the same promise.

> For he was looking forward to the city that has foundations, whose designer and builder is God. By faith Sarah herself received power to conceive, even when she was past the age, since she considered Him faithful who had promised. By faith Abraham, when he was tested, offered up Isaac, and he who had received the promises was in the act of offering up his only son, of whom it was said, "Through Isaac shall your offspring be named." He considered that God was able even to raise him from the dead, from which,

> figuratively speaking, he did receive him back (Hebrews 11:8–11, 17–19).

Abraham and Sarah's Muddy Buddy course was a continued, tested journey of faith. Four times the passage mentions "by faith." The first mention occurs when God called them to leave their family, friends, and comfortable home and go to a new land in Canaan. Abraham didn't even know where God was sending him, but he trusted the Lord to lead him into the unknown. Sarah trusted the Lord in her husband and stepped out in faith alongside him. Then, by Sarah's faith and God's mighty power, she conceived the promised child, Isaac, at age ninety-one![1] But their greatest test would come later when the Lord commanded Abraham to sacrifice his only beloved son, Isaac, the answer to God's promise.[2] Abraham trusted God even as he pulled the knife back. Abraham and Sarah had the assurance of things hoped for, the conviction of things not seen.[3] And by their faith, they would not quit, no matter the obstacles they endured.

But if He knew Abraham would not have to sacrifice his son in the end, why would God even ask him to do such a tragic, horrifying thing? What if God tested Abraham because he was in a child-centered marriage? Stay with me here. Abraham and Sarah had spent the past thirteen years waiting on God to fulfill His promise, all the while watching themselves grow older and older. They were not even supposed to be able to have a child, much less one through whom all the nations would be blessed and through whom would come generations numbering beyond the sand of the sea and the stars of the sky.[4] How could this be? Even Sarah laughed when God initially told them of the promised child.

After years of temptation to have their faith shaken, after years of pain as Sarah remained barren during their marriage, they finally received Isaac. What would their lives look like? What would their hearts look like? What if God was asking Abraham to surrender what he held most dear? What if his only son Isaac had become an idol? God was testing Abraham's loyalty, testing his affections to see whom he loved more—his Lord or his son, the Giver or the gift? Abraham received the promise. Now he was being asked to sacrifice the vision. By faith in God's character—he believed God could even raise his son from the dead—he was willing to offer his son out of a higher love for His Lord.[5] Abraham had the faith to trust and obey, and it was attributed to him as righteousness.[6]

Idolatry over a child could've been a central struggle in Abraham's and Sarah's lives. But marriages can also be destroyed when other things and people become the object of your affection over God, even if that object is your actual spouse. Perhaps idolatry of the spouse is what happened in the garden between Adam and Eve? He chose his wife over God, and look at the massive destruction, pain, and suffering it brought. Make no mistake, it's a big deal. Don't make your spouse into a god. You are pushing God out of the way while putting your spouse on a pedestal and setting him or her up for failure when he or she doesn't achieve your impossible expectations. Only a Christ-centered marriage works. Only God can occupy the throne of your heart.

Heartbreakingly, the casualties of divorce don't just plague the outside world; they also litter the field of ministry. An unhealthy marriage makes it impossible to be healthy in ministry or even work, especially over a long period of time. And your family pays the price. It can be a real challenge for men because we get so caught up in our work. We believe the lie that says our work defines us, our significance comes from our ability to provide. It becomes more important than anything else. We forget that our true calling in marriage is to give ourselves up for our wives, to lead them by serving them, and to love them as we nourish and cherish our own bodies.[7] When our God-given role gets skewed by our boss's or our culture's or our own expectations, disunity and destruction follows. I've seen the tremendous pain up close and personal with family members and friends. It is the number one need in our community and possibly the number one way the enemy will attack. Satan hates marriage because it is a picture of Christ and His redeemed Church.[8] He knows if he can divide your marriage, it can have a devastating effect on your children and your Kingdom purpose.

Like Abraham and Sarah, I had a rogue object of affection once, and it almost cost me my marriage. One night I came home to find my wife standing in the kitchen with four suitcases packed and waiting. Stephanie said, "I'm done. You're a great youth pastor, but you're not home enough to be a good husband and daddy. The kids never see you. Last month you were home only three nights. I won't do it by myself anymore. I'm taking the kids back home to Houston. Pick us or the church." Her gut punch was a reality check. No matter how defensive I felt, she was right. I had failed. We had already been through so much together—eleven years of marriage, three kids, the near-drowning of our firstborn daughter—but it didn't end up being trials or tribulations that nearly split us apart, it was ministry. The daily grind of life, the never-ending needs, the constant transitions and disrupting moves took their toll, and it was entirely my fault. I said yes to every opportunity offered. It's tempting to justify busyness for "God's sake." After all, it's His work, right? Just because it seems like God's work, that doesn't mean it is. I sacrificed my family on the altar of ministry but not because God asked me to.

After that conversation, I repented of my sin. I wasn't going to fail again by making another wrong decision. I'm grateful Stephanie loved me enough to confront me, and I'm still blown away by the fact that she forgave me. But confessing wasn't enough. It's easy to say words to put out the fire; it's hard to rebuild after the fire. I needed to restore our marriage. I needed to give myself up for her again, so she would come to trust me again through time and consistency. And by God's grace, she did. There's a reason why Jesus said to love God first and then love others.[9] How can we love correctly when we don't put the One who is Love first? Service to God must flow out of a healthy relationship with the Lord and your spouse. If you cross the finish line at work but not at home, do you really finish? Just like in the Muddy Buddy, you must stay the course side by side.

Due to my imperfections, I feel unqualified to give marriage advice. But please consider the valuable lessons I learned to sustain a healthy marriage. It doesn't happen on its own. If you want to blow through the red flags, I will summarize the four ways to wreck your marriage.

LOSE YOUR FIRST LOVE

Jesus is the greatest marriage counselor. He defines love as unselfish in John 15:3: "Greater love has no one than this, that someone lay down his life for his friends." Love always chooses the highest good of others. Let love be the defining attribute in your life. Marriage provides the greatest opportunity to learn how to unselfishly love. Love the way Jesus loved His bride, the Church, by serving. Imagine what would happen if you started every day by asking the Holy Spirit, "What's one practical thing I can do to serve my spouse?" and then followed through. Taking second place is a lifestyle, not a momentary decision. Train yourself to put others first. Make it a habit and put it into practice. You'll begin to look and lead more like Jesus.

Jesus also gives great advice on how you can reignite your first love with Him in Revelation 2:4–5: "But I have this against you, that you have abandoned the love you had at first. Remember therefore from where you have fallen; repent, and do the works you did at first." Our works and service come out as a natural overflow from our love for God. The same truth in ministry applies to relationships. Every couple does the same first works during the "honeymoon stage." Flowers. Custom playlists. Doors opened. Interlocked hands. Long hugs. Handwritten poems. Lots of kissing and dates. Go back and do that stuff again and again. It's amazing how a little romance will breathe new life and excitement into a relationship. The grass isn't greener on the other side. The grass is greener wherever you water it.

I'll never forget the day I met Stephanie Edwards. I was a junior in college and Shara, my sister, asked if I was ready to meet my future wife. Who could say no? Eager to meet, hopefully, the love of my life, I quickly followed her into the cafeteria where she introduced me to her friend, Stephanie. It was love at first sight—for one of us.

My only chance as a guy with a ridiculous mullet and a pathetic excuse for a beard was for her to know me. I had a "Beauty and the Beast" hunch that if Stephanie could just look past the outside and get to know me, she could learn to love me. I went to every single one of her home volleyball games and cheered louder than anyone every time she bumped, set, or spiked the ball. I moved so I could sit right behind her in the only class we shared. Since she didn't have her own vehicle, I stalked her during her free time and offered her rides to anywhere she wanted to go. Finally, she said yes to a first date. Unfortunately, it wasn't a first date with me but with my roommate!

Considering her worth it, I broke the bro code and didn't give up until I was the one who placed a ring on her finger. With her contagious joy, smile that lit up every room, positive attitude, gift of mercy for the marginalized, patience with children, and strong devotional life with the Lord, Stephanie was the most beautiful person I'd ever laid eyes on. And I still feel that way about her today. Her character amplifies her outer beauty. I chose to fix my gaze on her, and I refused to take my eyes off her until I was hers and she was mine.

Time wins. Not just quality time but large amounts of quality time. Never take each other for granted. Stephanie and I have a standing weekly date. Our favorite excursion is riding my Triumph Scrambler motorcycle up Highway 16 and deep into the Hill Country to a spot along a Texan-style, "lazy" river called Medina River. Surrounded by the gentle buzz of insects and the quiet shush of the meandering river, lined with tall and majestic Cypress trees, we put up our hammocks, take naps, and if I get lucky, we cuddle.

Intentions are not good enough. Follow through. Make time for each other because if you don't, everything will revolve around your job or the children, and you'll crash when the kids leave or you switch jobs or you retire. Place your weekly date on the calendar and make it a priority. Once every few months, surprise your spouse with a romantic, overnight getaway. Get creative and have fun! Think about what your spouse would like. If you really want to spice things up, take it to another level and go back to that honeymoon stage. Remember your first love and go to bed naked seven nights in a row. Heck, go for a month! #GTBN.

STAY OUT FIVE NIGHTS A WEEK

Church planting is possibly one of the most challenging ministry assignments, but it saved my marriage. Planting a church meant I could set my own schedule.

While preparing for a career change after Stephanie gave me a second chance, I read *Confessions of a Pastor* by Craig Groeschel.[10] He revealed a core value that totally shifted my point of view and brought my marriage back into alignment. He recommended making the immovable decision to, no matter what, stay home from ministry five nights a week. I was shocked. I didn't think that was allowed in ministry. Still feeling unsure about this too-good-to-be-true possibility, I casually ran the idea past Stephanie. To my surprise, she agreed to give it a shot. It would turn out to be one of the best ministry decisions we ever made because here we are, ten years later, keeping our promise to each other and enjoying a healthy, balanced marriage *and* ministry.

It wasn't all roses. Saying yes to Stephanie meant saying no to ministry—over and over again. In the early years of Gateway, it meant declining many invitations to parties and dinners. It was hard but worth it. God honored our ministry sacrifice because we were putting each other first. It also helped to keep our church philosophy simple by not allowing extraneous events or programs to fill our schedules. By streamlining our ministries to only include the essential, we found extra time to pour into our families and develop a desire for quality instead of quantity when serving our church family. Seeing the fruit in our own lives, we made it an expectation for our directors and pastors to honor the same core value of staying home five nights a week. We're so grateful we belong to the most amazing church family, one that respects and even encourages this boundary.

Work might not be the greatest threat for you. When you examine how you spend your free time, what happens whenever you have that "extra" time in your schedule? Are you tempted to fill it with all sorts of things except your family? The truth is, giving your extra time to a hobby, a passion for fitness, or entertainment is not bad in and of itself. But you must realize that by filling it with things like that, you're spending too much time on yourself. I'm not saying God doesn't want you to enjoy those things. But follow the convictions of the Holy Spirit and listen to your spouse. God wants you to have priorities. He is a God of order. He's designed you for them and expects you to steward the time He gives you for fruitful labor. Guard your calendar, or others and other things will control it.

NEVER GO TO COUNSELING

The third way to wreck your marriage is to never ask for help when things get tough. Where is your greatest source of help? It's made clear in the Word of God: "I lift up my eyes to the hills. From where does my help come? My help comes from the Lord, who made heaven and earth" (Psalm 121:1–2). Grab a hold of your spouse and pray. Cry out to God for help. The Holy Spirit is available every moment of every day to guide you to truth. Prayer softens the heart and the attitude and the tone of your inner voice. It places you in the posture necessary to hear from the Lord and prepares you to be slow to speak and quick to listen. May the Lord be who you consult first when you encounter the obstacles ahead.

God offers help through His perfect, wise counsel. Busyness, insecurity, and finances are not good enough reasons to avoid counseling. Just as a garden will become overgrown and wild without regular pruning, every couple needs regular counseling "checkups" for tweaks and adjustments before the inevitable happens and crisis overwhelms the marriage. Pastor Rick Warren says it's better to go into debt from marriage counseling than to pay lawyer fees.

Stephanie and I are grateful for the marriage counseling we received during our difficult times. We've had more than our fair share of weeds to pull, but there was one particularly deep-rooted disagreement that seemed to crop up often: conflict regarding the method of correcting our children. We were raised on opposite ends of the parenting spectrum. Stephanie was the princess who was never disciplined. I was the rebel who got spanked, belt-whipped, and lit up every week until I was a teenager. And believe me, I needed every one. Stephanie and I needed a wise, godly, unbiased, outside perspective, so we asked for help. Resolving conflict requires humility, giving each other the benefit of the doubt, honesty, healthy communication, and a commitment not to give up on each other. Before things go nuclear, get help.

EXPECT PERFECTION

Honestly, anything good I bring to my marriage was inspired by my parents. They're not perfect, but their faithfulness left a powerful legacy. We celebrated their fortieth anniversary on the island of Maui. They gave me the honor of officiating an intimate ceremony as they renewed their vows. Mom wanted it to be perfect. She chose a quaint, little, white chapel overlooking the ocean during sunset. The view was beyond belief. At the front of the chapel where we gathered, Mom had carefully arranged tall, fragrant, exotic floral arrangements that were gently cradled in ceramic vases. Then, right in the middle of this gorgeous, peaceful ceremony, disaster struck. Dad accidentally knocked one of the vases over. Powdery chunks of ceramic exploded all over the ground, water gushed out everywhere, flowers scattered, and the perfectness of the moment shattered into a thousand, irretrievable pieces, along with Mom's expectations. Obviously, she was shaken up at first, but then she realized it was a great metaphor for their relationship. The moment was redeemed, and the ceremony concluded with smiles, celebration by all, and maybe some good-natured laughter.

Marriage, like any relationship, gets messy at times. You're not perfect, so don't expect perfection. Conflict is not a matter of "if" but "when." Redeem the moments of failure and human error. How you respond to the mess will determine how you finish.

Sometimes you don't realize the gravity of expecting perfection from your partner. Sometimes you don't see it for what it truly is. If you expect perfection, you don't understand the reality of the fallen nature of humanity, and—like me, Abraham, and Sarah—you will be tempted with an improper object of affection, an idol. If left unchecked, the pursuit of this idol will lead to disappointment. Don't make your spouse an idol. Adjust expectations and keep them off the throne of your heart. Instead, direct your gaze to Jesus and constantly forgive as Christ forgave you.

On the other hand, just as you can treasure each other too much, you can also neglect each other. Never ever take each other for granted. You are not promised tomorrow. Pray together and for each other. Make a list of everything you appreciate about your spouse then make another list of all your favorite memories together. When things get tough and you're tempted to quit, pull out those lists and give thanks to the One who put the two of you together. A grateful heart will get you through anything.

And finally, above all, never quit on each other. Except for Himself, your spouse is the greatest gift God has given you. And you are a gift from God to your spouse, so act like one. Stay committed. Enjoy the rewards from longevity in a Christ-centered marriage. Leave a legacy of faithfulness for your children and your grandchildren. Their heritage of faith will be a crown upon your head. Words are powerful, but it's not enough to just declare your love. Instead, live your life out as an example of godly unity, and your love for each other will never fade. Remember, God put you in your spouse's life because He knew you'd be better together.

6

PASS THE BATON

ISAAC

Create your legacy, and pass the baton.

Billie Jean King

"Where is Hannah Grace?" my wife asked.

In just four short words, her voice rose to a panic when she couldn't locate our three-year-old daughter. "Somebody!" she screamed. "Please! She is wearing a brown swimsuit and a pink bow. Help find her!"

I'll never forget those screams.

I ran through the crowd to the edge of the deep end of the pool where fifty people were gathered. I leaned over the edge, and my heart pounded as I searched the murky water. A pain worse than anything I'd ever felt gripped my heart. Where was my baby girl?

Suddenly, a man on the other side of the pool dove into the deep end. But when he came up out of the water holding my Hannah, any sense of hope vanished. He placed her tiny, limp body in my arms. The pain became terror. I realized her arms were bare. She must have stripped off her floaties so she could swim like the big kids. She wasn't breathing.

No parent should ever see their child look so lifeless.

A woman took her and began performing CPR as I yelled for the lifeguard. I watched, stricken, as Hannah Grace coughed up a liter of water. Her little eyes rolled back and forth and then…nothing.

I wasn't going to wait for an ambulance.

I carried her at a run to my car and sped to the hospital. With my unconscious daughter on my lap I begged the Lord to help her. Suddenly, the car pulled hard to the right. I got out and saw that the front, left tire was flat. It became personal. Whether it was an attack or not, I rebuked the enemy. I drove the last few miles with a flat tire, refusing to give up.

After parking at the front doors, I carried Hannah into the emergency room. They checked her vitals, placed an IV in her arm, and rushed us in an ambulance to the children's hospital. They told me to pray. Her blood oxygen levels were very low, and they were unsure of how much damage had been done to her brain.

Watching her lying there on the gurney, I remembered the Sunday I dedicated her to God. I realized in hindsight her dedication was more of a ritual than anything else.

Right then and there I rededicated her in my heart. I desperately told God my daughter belonged to Him. She was His, and only He could save her.

We spent seven days in the ICU. Every fifteen minutes, I pleaded for God to save Hannah as I watched her breathe, paced by her bed, and kissed my favorite little freckle on the right side of her nose. I prayed over my daughter like I'd never prayed before in my life.

God heard us. Hannah Grace made a miraculous, full recovery! The doctor said if she had swallowed any more water or hadn't gotten air right when she did, she could have died or suffered significant brain damage.

The Lord redeemed that moment. Life can be unexpectedly short. Don't take it for granted. We are not promised tomorrow.[1]

Often, I walk into my daughter's room to kiss that same little freckle on her nose and give God thanks for sparing her life. Apart from the Lord and my wife, the lives of my three children are my most valuable treasures. The weight and responsibility of raising them to love the Lord became more important after this miracle. My goal and my calling are not only to protect them from worldly dangers but also to prepare them to face the temptations and trials of this world. As their father, my number one priority is to pass the baton of faith to my children.

The next endurance runner mentioned in Hebrews 11 did just that.

"By faith Isaac blessed Jacob and Esau concerning things to come" (Hebrews 11:20, NKJV).

Isaac has already been discussed as a son, so let's talk about him as a father. Out of everything Isaac did, the Holy Spirit selected one thing, recorded in Genesis 27, to give him a place among the endurance runners: Isaac won at home. He was marked by faith because he blessed his sons. Initially, he may have been deceived by his son Jacob, but Isaac followed through and blessed his other son, Esau, as well.[2]

Isaac's blessing over Esau is often forgotten. Even though the two blessings were very different, in a way they accomplished the same thing. By faith Isaac blessed Esau, prophesying he would eventually be freed from the yoke of his brother even though Esau had thrown away God's birthright like trash—trading an eternal blessing for a bowl of soup.[3] Isaac's blessing over Esau was in faith because he believed the promise God gave Adam and Eve in Genesis 3: A savior would come to redeem even Esau's descendants.[4] He also believed the promise given to his father, Abraham: "And in your off spring shall all the nations of the earth be blessed."[5] *All* the nations, including those of Esau, would be blessed.

His other son was no saint either. Despite Jacob's wicked deception, God took Jacob's evil and used it for good through His mercy and grace.[6] By faith, Isaac spoke God's blessing over his younger son, declaring he would receive benefits from the earth, receive the favor of people, rule over his brother, and receive a lordship to be fully realized through Jesus. God took both sons, one a careless nonbeliever and the other a liar and a cheat, as a foreshadowing of His plan to save both Gentiles and Hebrews, to display a beautiful picture of His redeeming love.

Through these blessings, Isaac passed to both his sons the traditional promise given to him by Abraham. He continued the vision God gave for their family: "I will be your God. Be the priest who continues to worship Me and teach the laws of God." This "blessing" was more than a dying father saying goodbye or hoping for the best for his children. Isaac spoke boldly as a prophet proclaiming their descendants would be saved by the Lord.

What if you truly considered the weight of Isaac's example? You are called to make disciples of your biological *and* spiritual children. Disciple the children you personally parent and friends who become spiritual children. The call of discipleship includes those in your home, neighborhood, classroom, and work place. You are anointed by God to speak a blessing of faith over them.

These life-giving words will have more weight than you realize when you become intentional about raising your children to fear God, to believe His words. Your children need you to disciple, train, and lead them. Proverbs 22:6 says, "Train up a child in the way he should go; even when he is old he will not depart from it." This is your greatest responsibility and your greatest honor. Many parents today are not sure how to train up their children because it was not modeled well for them by their own parents. So how can you come alongside them and bear this burden without taking it from them?

If you don't disciple your children, the world will. Commercials and social media are targeting your children with a view from the world. Disagreeing with mainstream, cultural values results in persecution, judgment, and accusations of being intolerant and even abusive. The truth is that discipline without love is abuse, but parenting without discipline is also abuse.[7] The Bible instructs us not to conform to cultural norms when they are contrary to the Word of God.[8] Who will you follow? God or the shifting winds of culture?[9]

In 2008, the Americans fumbled the baton in a preliminary race, eliminating them from advancing in the Olympic 400-meter relays they had performed perfectly in the past. The United States track and field relay team failed to successfully hand off the third and final baton, costing them their heavily favored gold medal. All the time spent training was lost because of a failure to pass the baton.

Joshua led the children of Israel into the Promised Land. However, Scripture reveals the next generation after did not know the Lord. Joshua successfully received the baton from Moses, but he failed to pass it on. Choose to be the parent who passes the baton to your children.

So where do you start? Understanding discipleship, the method through which you can pass on the baton, begins with Jesus. If Jesus is divine in His character and teachings, He also must be divine in His methods. What was His method of discipleship? As you discover the essential truths in the next three essential passages, never stray from them. They are life and refreshment to your soul.[10]

> Go therefore and make disciples of all the nations, baptizing them in the name of the Father and of the Son and of the Holy Spirit, teaching them to observe all things that I have commanded you; and lo, I am with you always, even to the end of the age (Matthew 28:19–20).

> Hear, O Israel: The Lord our God, the Lord is one. You shall love the Lord your God with all your heart and with all your soul and with all your might. And these words that I command you today shall be on your heart. You shall teach them diligently to your children, and shall talk of them when you sit in your house, and when you walk by the way, and when you lie down, and when you rise. You shall bind them as a sign on your hand, and they shall be as frontlets between your eyes. You shall write them on the doorposts of your house and on your gates (Deuteronomy 6:4–9).

> And what you have heard from me in the presence of many witnesses entrust to faithful men, who will be able to teach others also (2 Timothy 2:2).

Please consider a simple "in, up, and out" approach to help your children become devoted followers of Jesus, so when they leave the nest they won't spiritually drift. Every healthy small group lives an inward (relational), upward (spiritual), and outward (missional) expression. These discipleship principles are the same tools for helping your friends become devoted followers of Jesus.

IN

Families who play together stay together. They have real relationships. Jesus started His earthly discipleship journey by inviting twelve friends into His inner circle of relationships. He poured into their lives for three years before he passed the baton. Imagine the time they spent together in fellowship—traveling, fishing, building stuff, and sharing meals together. Discipleship can't happen apart from friendship. It is intimacy over information, relationship over religion. It must be more than content transfer filling in the blanks and informing others what they should believe. Write down the five most life-changing sermons you've ever heard and compare your list to the five most influential people in your life. You'll quickly see how important relationships are to discipleship. Sermons only happen once a week. Whoever spends the most time in relationship wins the heart.

For the last ten years, I've made every effort to tip the scales to the other side because I'd already found out the hard way that there was no relationship when I wasn't present. Make weekly family fun nights a priority. Play games together. Some of our favorite memories are of being silly together. God invented humor. Love and laughter plow the soil of hearts.

Family time is so important, but the most valuable time you can spend with someone is face-to-face in a monthly one-on-one. My favorite part of skiing with my kids is the uninterrupted fifteen minutes on the chairlift. Each of your children has a unique love language. This becomes the time to demonstrate this love to them. Ask good questions and listen with your heart. Your child will not remember everything you say, but he or she will remember the time you spent with him or her.

If you desire your children to live with a sense of adventure, expose them to a thrilling lifestyle early on. When we didn't have enough money for a Disney vacation, we made it a priority to tent camp on a shoestring budget. This gave way to our favorite activities of white water rafting and climbing fourteeners[11] together.

UP

Families who pray together stay together. They have real devotions. Jesus instructs you in the Great Commission to teach your children everything He commands and to baptize them in water. At a time when there were no Butterfinger candy bars, it was common for a first-century rabbi to place honey on the lips of his "talmud," which is the Hebrew word for "learner." He would also recite the following from Psalm 119:103: "How sweet are your words to my taste, sweeter than honey to my mouth!" Just like Jesus, he desired his followers to develop a hunger for God and His Word.

Your children must see your love for the Lord. You modeling a strong devotional life is one of your greatest gifts to them. Let them catch you kneeling in your secret place or having the Bible open on your lap. Your vision as a parent, your top priority, must be to transfer your child's dependence from you to the Lord.

Family devotions must be a priority. Three mornings a week before school, my daughters and I study Scripture with the S.O.A.P.[12] method or read a proverb. My younger son Bryce and I discovered the Action Bible. It transforms Bible stories into fun and powerful comic strips. I even use a ridiculous, sidekick puppet turtle named Crush to keep things silly, fun, and interesting. I'm willing to look foolish because I desperately want my children to love and engage with God's word at the youngest possible age. Go out and get a Bible that works for your family, and let your children choose a puppet to become the newest member of your family. Use the personalized methods God will inspire for you and your family to explain what Jesus did on the cross. Don't wait for Sunday. Take communion together. Teach the important fundamentals of your faith. Encourage your family to have a strong devotional life on their own, and see the growth God brings to your children's lives.

OUT

Families who serve together stay together. Every member of the family has real responsibility. Jesus didn't say, "Some of you go make disciples." He said, "Go and make disciples." But he didn't send them without training them first and modeling how to minister and pray for the sick and take care of the outsiders, the rejected, the widows, and the orphans. Later, when the early Church in Jerusalem came under persecution, the Lord used it to send his followers out. And the Church exploded with global growth. There must be an outward focus for spiritual growth. Volunteer at church and serve those outside the four walls. Watch what happens in your children when they catch your passion to help those in need.

A lot is riding on your decision to practice what you preach. But even if you do model how to go and make disciples, it is impossible to lead in a healthy way if your family does not participate along with you. If your family isn't passionately serving with you, don't wait to have a talk about it to discover why. You may be discouraged because you didn't "train up" your children in a way that most reflects the method of Jesus. But don't let the enemy bring condemnation or discouragement. Start praying for your children now and allow the Holy Spirit to lead you.

The Lord cares more about your children than you do. If your daughter has lost her way, know she is not forgotten. Jesus tells a story of a lost son who leaves home to pursue a selfish and sinful lifestyle.[13] The loving father never left the home to rescue his son or shelter him from the consequences of his rebellion. When the foolish son was convicted and then repented of his sin, he made his way back home. The father was waiting on the front porch when he saw his lost son in the distance. Immediately, he took off running and embraced his son and threw a giant party.

The Lord's love compels like a parent who has lost his own daughter, as I lost my Hannah Grace in the deep end of the pool that day. "Where is she? Help. She has a pink bow and is wearing a brown bathing suit. She is in great need. Please help find her. Pink bow. Brown swimsuit. She must be found." Never give up hope. Never stop praying. Never stop loving. God is able to bring her home.

7

FIGHT

JACOB

Better to fight for something than live for nothing.

GENERAL GEORGE PATTON

SPANDEX.

Unless you're a serious athlete, you don't wear it. Ever. Breaking "Man Rule Number Five" is a sure-fire way to lose a Man Card while simultaneously pushing the boundaries of public decency.

You know where I'm going with this by now.

Years ago, while training for my first triathlon, I paid for the race, did my research, and created a nutrition and training plan. I'm an optimist. Surely, I could swim a half mile without resorting to what every other triathlete wore, right?

As the weeks passed and the race date approached, I finally admitted to myself I couldn't do it anymore. I'd tried practice laps in the pool with a regular swimsuit, but the constant drag from my board shorts sapped my energy and tugged at my forward motion like a parachute.

After much deliberation, I made the decision.

Early one morning, I arrived at the Sherwood Harmon Recreation Pool the moment it opened, thinking the chances were slim that anyone would see me when I...unveiled. Words can't express how nervous I was in the locker room as I struggled into the black, bikini Speedo. I started to pray.

Please, God, don't let anyone be in the pool.

Even though I was sure I'd be alone, I slid my board shorts over the indecent display, just in case, and walked out into the pool area. To my horror, a group of elderly women were gathered in the shallow end doing aerobic exercises.

Seriously, God?

Like a junior high school boy at his first dance, I had to be as far away from these ladies as possible. So, I gingerly walked over to the last lane on the opposite side of the pool. I stretched for ten minutes, hoping their class would end.

It didn't.

There are times in a man's life when he must "bite the bullet."

I tried my best to hold up my towel like a curtain while I slipped my board shorts off. I got one leg out but accidentally dropped my towel, showcasing all my glory.

Let me tell you, nothing hides in Spandex. Every nook and cranny was revealed to all.

One lady, God bless her, shouted, "Oh, honey, take it all off!"

In a moment of panic, I purposely fell into the pool and stayed underwater while scrambling to get the other leg out of my shorts. When I finally raised my head above the water, I was met with cackles, hoots, and hollers echoing off the cement walls. The noise was deafening. In a complete state of shame and humiliation, I quickly escaped back under the water.

Thanks, God.

This was retaliation. I broke the code and never should've worn Spandex in a place where women and children gather.

I surfaced, pulled my towel into the water to cover up, and exited with zero dignity.

Sure, breaking a Man Rule wasn't a sin, but I still felt the sting of shame that follows it. Just like Adam and Eve in the garden covering up their nakedness, shame and sin go hand in hand. The embarrassment I endured at the pool prevented me from training. Don't let shame or sin hinder your training as an endurance runner. If you don't train well, if you don't fight, you won't finish well.

Few Hebrew endurance runners fought their way to victory like Jacob. Chapter eleven records how he crossed the finish line in triumph. But at the beginning of his race, things were different. Jacob stumbled off the starting blocks and then tripped and fell. He scraped and crawled his way to the finish line. First, he cheated his brother, Esau, out of his firstborn birthright. Then, as if cheating his brother wasn't bad enough, when his father, Isaac, lay on his deathbed, Jacob gave in to temptation again. At his mom's insistence, he followed through with a deceitful plan to take advantage of his ailing father and once again destroy his brother's future. God wasn't deceived. After Jacob's deception, an enraged Esau planned to murder his younger twin brother in retaliation. In fear, Jacob ran. But over the course of his life, this cheat and liar must have been seriously humbled to cross the finish line like he did: "By faith Jacob, when dying, blessed each of the sons of Joseph, bowing in worship over the head of his staff" (Hebrews 11:21).

The day of Jacob's death was filled with prophetic blessings over his sons and grandsons. Jacob was sick and knew the time had come for him to be "gathered to his people,"[1] but he called in Joseph, Manasseh, and Ephraim first. Knowing his time was short, Jacob made a final request of Joseph to not leave his body in Egypt, the land of captivity, and to bring it to the Promised Land. When Joseph promised to honor his request, Jacob exerted his last bit of strength to get out of bed, bow, and, leaning on his staff for support, worship the Lord in faith that one day he would be carried home, the very place he had once run from.[2]

So, what happened between these two, contrasting bookends of his life? What made Jacob stop cheating and deceiving his way into blessings and instead learn how to fight for them the right way, to seek until it was given, to knock until it was opened?[3] Jacob stopped searching for the gift and sought the Giver. He stopped running away. He spent most of his life weaseling his way into blessings, but now he was willing to truthfully fight face-to-face and suffer to receive victory. Jacob submitted himself into the Lord's hands and wrestled with God.

> And Jacob was left alone. And a Man wrestled with him until the breaking of the day. When the Man saw that He did not prevail against Jacob, He touched his hip socket, and Jacob's hip was put out of joint as He wrestled with him. Then He said, "Let Me go, for the day has broken."
>
> But Jacob said, "I will not let You go unless You bless me."
>
> And He said to him, "What is your name?"
>
> And he said, "Jacob."

> Then He said, "Your name shall no longer be called Jacob, but Israel; for you have striven with God and with men, and have prevailed."
>
> Then Jacob asked Him, "Please tell me Your name."
>
> But He said, "Why is it that you ask My name?" And there He blessed him.
>
> So Jacob called the name of the place Peniel, saying, "For I have seen God face to face, and yet my life has been delivered." The sun rose upon him as he passed Penuel, limping because of his hip (Genesis 32:24–31).

Wrestling is exhausting. Most can't go beyond fifteen minutes. It took enduring faith for Jacob to fight God all night. The Lord used that night to develop Jacob's perseverance and faith because He knew Jacob would need that growth. The bigger the race, the bigger the temptation.

The enemy is a thief waiting to steal the faith you need to cross the finish line. If you're struggling with a stronghold of sin, discover how to fight.[4] Wrestle with God. Work out your salvation with fear and trembling. No one values a medal that is just handed over. It's the fight that makes the victory sweet, but there's only One who can reward you with the imperishable wreath.[5] Submit and place yourself in the hands of the Commander of the Lord's army,[6] the One to whom the battle belongs,[7] and then never let go. James 4:8 says to draw near to God and He will draw near to you. Make the choice not to run from shame and consequences. Fight. You are as victorious as you want to be.

STOP RUNNING

The first apartment Stephanie and I rented in the small town of McKinney, Texas, was only $300 a month, but there was a catch. We weren't the only residents; the entire complex was filled to the brim with roaches. Every time we turned on the kitchen light, they would scatter, skittering across the linoleum to hide. Most of the time I could tell where they'd gone. But whenever I moved a table or box or shoes, they hid in another place. We're like that, aren't we? We try to run from God and keep sinning, but He still sees us.

When Adam and Eve sinned, they tried to run and hide. God asked them two questions: "Where are you?"[8] and "What have you done?"[9] God is still asking these questions today. He is not asking them because He doesn't know their answers but because He is giving us the opportunity to stop running. Will you face the brutal facts of your sin and how it is destroying your life, relationship with God, and witness?

HIS GRACE IS STRONGER

Once, I heard a powerful story I've never forgotten. I don't know if the story, told by F. W. Boreham, is fictional or not, but it certainly made an impression on me.

Long ago in nineteenth-century London, a young, foolish girl decided to disobey her parents and play with matches. One evening she lit a match, and this time the flame rapidly grew out of her control. It ignited the drapes and soon the entire top floor of her home was filled with smoke and fire. The girl tried to make her way to her parent's room, but the smoke was too intense.

She discovered later her parents did not survive.

Somehow, through the poisonous, choking fog of smoke, the little girl made her way to a hallway window and pried it open, using her dress to shield her hands from the heated metal. When she leaned her head out to breathe fresh air, smoke poured out around her. She saw neighbors shouting and pointing from the street.

Some men tried to go through the front door to rescue her, but the handle was too hot and the heat too intense. One man saw what was happening and noticed a lead pipe leading up to the top floor of the house. It also passed the little girl's window. He found a way to rescue her. The heat of the pipe hit his hands before he even grasped the lead. But he climbed anyway. He had to save her. Skin peeled and flesh sizzled as hand went over hand. He kept reminding himself of how afraid the little girl must be and how he was her only chance of survival. Finally, he reached her. Trying not to breathe in the smoke, he placed her on his back and made his way down, this time enduring even more pain because of his raw hands and the extra weight from the little girl.

The neighbors cheered when they reached the bottom, but the man and little girl needed immediate medical attention. The neighbors took both of them to the hospital because of their severe burns. Weeks later, the authorities and councilmen called a town meeting to decide what to do with the foolish girl who played with matches. Before turning her over to a state orphanage, they asked if anyone would volunteer to take care of this girl because her parents had perished in the flames. The room was silent as people looked around. After several moments, one hand wrapped in bandages and gauze raised from the back of the room. It was the man who had climbed the lead pipe and risked so much to save the foolish girl.

Jesus endured the cross to save you from your sin. He loves you that much. Your sin may feel big, but grace is bigger. Praise God that "where sin increased, grace abounded all the more" (Romans 5:20). The power in His blood and resurrection is enough to forgive and set you free. He fought for you. Fight for Him. This story also illustrates how Jesus' care for you does not end when you receive His redemption.

CONFESS AND REPENT

When I was in eighth grade, a classmate introduced me to his brother's drawer full of porn magazines. It shattered my innocence. Every few months, I would succumb to temptation and spiral into lustful thoughts, plunging me into a continuous cycle of sin, shame, and confession. I was broken to the point of despair and mourned over my sin. After confessing to the Lord, I felt the Holy Spirit lead me to confess it to friends. It was one of the most humbling and difficult moments of my life. This confession and accountability led to victory over sin.

Sin thrives in darkness. Sin is missing the mark and a rebellious departure from God's character. If you don't take sin seriously, you don't need a Savior. Get help. Don't keep it a secret. Turn away from sin. Freedom comes through repentance. Confessing and repenting breaks its power over you. Don't be afraid. Don't run like Jacob did. Fight! No matter what it takes. The Lord already knows what you've done and

He still doesn't condemn you, so don't let fear and pride prevent you from finding freedom in Christ.[10] As 1 John 1:9 proclaims, the Lord is faithful and just to forgive your sins when you confess them.

LOVE JESUS MORE THAN SIN

When my children were little, they obeyed me because they were happy about a reward or afraid of a punishment. They didn't want to obey, but they feared discipline more than they loved rebellion. As they grew, something changed. They began to obey me because they loved me. They recognized who I was as a loving father, and that love is what drove their obedience. Do we recognize what God has done for us? Praise God for what He's done, and your life and your worship will light a fire you won't be able to contain. Obey as an overflow of your love for your Lord and watch as the gleaming lure of sin becomes strangely dim in the light of His glory and grace.[11]

PUT ON THE ARMOR OF GOD

Wake up each morning and ask God to help you put on your armor. The apostle Paul writes in Ephesians 6:13–17,

> Therefore, take up the whole armor of God, that you may be able to withstand in the evil day, and having done all, to stand firm. Stand therefore, having fastened on the belt of truth, and having put on the breastplate of righteousness, and, as shoes for your

> feet, having put on the readiness given by the gospel of peace. In all circumstances take up the shield of faith, with which you can extinguish all the flaming darts of the evil one; and take the helmet of salvation, and the sword of the Spirit, which is the word of God.

PLACE BOUNDARIES

You are responsible for guarding your mind and heart: "Guard your heart above all else, for it determines the course of your life" (Proverbs 4:23, NLT). Be aware of the enemy's tactics. Temptation comes when you are H.A.L.T.: Hungry, Angry, Lonely, or Tired. Any combination of these things can be dangerous. Be ready. Safeguard every media device. Surround yourself with friends who build you up. Don't be alone with someone of the opposite sex you aren't married to.

FIGHT

During the same conference where I discovered the revolutionizing S.O.A.P. method, I rented a bike one afternoon and went for a ride. Exhausted and hungry, I walked into a restaurant. Shortly after finding a seat at a table, an attractive woman leaned over and asked, "Do you want company tonight?" This is the only time in my life something like this has ever happened to me.

Shock reverberated through me and a desperate prayer surfaced: *Help me, Lord!* In that very instant the Holy Spirit reminded me of 1 Corinthians 6:18, which instructs us to run from sexual sin. I had to get out of there. I blurted out, "I love my wife! I love my wife!" and ran out of the restaurant back to my hotel room without stopping, locking the door behind me as if she were chasing me.

I didn't eat dinner that night, but I'm so grateful God's grace was stronger. True character is revealed in your greatest temptation. If it's an area of weakness, you can either run before you sin, or you'll be faced with the temptation to run after you sin. But thanks be to God He doesn't leave you in a state of constant defense. In time, the Lord will make you strong enough to go on the offensive, to stand and fight. He will develop your faith and humility so that you will submit yourself to God and resist the devil.[12] Fight like Jesus did in the wilderness against the devil. He went on the offensive and used His Sword, the Word of God. Three times the enemy tempted Him, and three times He responded with, "It is written."[13] Jesus gives you the same authority, grace, and power to overcome any attack of the enemy. Make the decision now to do what is right in public or in private. Be honest. Be humble. Allow the Holy Spirit to guide you with His moral compass. Never quit. Your biggest breakthroughs happen after an intense battle. Finish the race with endurance and keep the faith.[14] Step up and fight!

8

TRIALS POSSESS GREAT PURPOSE

JOSEPH

If you're going through hell, keep going.

Anonymous

Swim 2.4 miles.

Ride a bike for 112 miles.

Run 26.2 miles.

This is the IRONMAN TRIATHLON. It's the big daddy of long-distance triathlons. It's also the race Julie Moss and her heartbreaking, second-place finish made famous in 1982. I was just a young kid when I saw the dramatic ending unfold on TV, but her battle to cross that finish line is still etched on my mind. I remember watching her fall, crawl, and scrape her way toward the finish line for two miles, only to be passed by a competitor seconds before crossing. Her struggle had a huge impact on me. And I couldn't help but think of her as I stood at the edge of Lake Placid in New York during the cold, pre-dawn hours, about to compete in my own IRONMAN TRIATHLON. Would the months of training and careful consideration for proper nutrition pay off?

The race began at 7:00 a.m., and the mandatory cut-off was midnight. Incredibly, I crossed the lake on time and didn't suffer too many kicks to the head, but the bike ride would prove challenging. Seventy miles into the race on hilly pavement, my rear tire pressure became low. Later, the gears stopped functioning properly because of a failure in my rear derailleur.

But the mechanical issue I faced on the bike was nothing compared to the suffering I experienced at the end of the run. As I fought my way toward the finish line, I passed athlete after athlete collapsed on the side of the road, grim reminders of Julie Moss who were like chilling prophecies should I also give in to the temptation to give up. As I ran the final four miles down Riverside Drive, a volunteer at a rest stop told me a former medal winner from the 1980 Winter Olympics was standing ahead at the turn near the ski jumps. Several minutes later, as I approached, I watched other runners touch his medal while he spurred us on to finish strong. His encouragement was the motivation I needed to endure the final few miles necessary to earn a medal and hear a voice declare on a cranked sound system, "You are an IRONMAN!"

The Lord helped me finish. But no matter the blessing of the Lord, the training, or the dialed-in nutrition, I never expected a painless, long-distance race. Anything can go wrong. You can still blow a tire or break a chain. You can still battle discouragement and the temptation to collapse just a few miles from the finish line. It's the same in life, isn't it? So why are we surprised when we suffer or when things go wrong? Trials happen no matter who you are. Jesus even promises we will endure temptations, persecution, and trials. So, how will you respond during the suffering of obstacles? What attitude will you choose when God doesn't answer your prayers according to your preference? Your willingness to endure through the suffering must be determined before you start, or you'll cave in to the temptation to take the easy way out.

Everyone loves the start and the finish, but it's the grind in the middle that wins the medal and makes the athlete. My suffering during the IRONMAN pales in comparison to real-life trials.

"Unfortunately, it's not a cyst. It's a tumor we have to surgically remove."

A...tumor?

My doctor pointed to an MRI scan in the small office, but I couldn't concentrate on anything else he said. The idea of surgery and the very real possibility of cancer took over every other thought.

Why, God?

We were just months away from moving out of the movie theater and into our first permanent home as a church. Shouldn't this be a time of triumph and victory? Not even close. Not only did I have a tumor, the place where it chose to reside was no joke. Imagine the worst place possible. It kept me off my bike for six months. The timing was another damper on circumstances as Stephanie and I had already planned our twentieth anniversary trip to Jamaica, but surgery had to be done as soon as possible. We scheduled it for the day after we returned home.

It was hard to enjoy our anniversary trip or the upcoming opening of the building with the surgery looming. After it was over, the time between the announcement and the biopsy results was a grind. My friend Google was no help. Stay away from him at all costs. The enemy and my flesh were no help either. As a preacher, it's a lot more fun to preach trust than to live it out from a pit. The unknown is the breeding ground for anxiety. The temptation to worry was there, but ultimately it couldn't win.

Praise be to God this great trial became a sweet victory. The tumor was benign. However, the true victory wasn't physical, it was spiritual. The work the Lord did in me during that time was priceless. The Lord carried me, broken and humbled. It was His presence during the dark nights that gave me peace. Quoting Scripture in the hospital room moments before surgery birthed joy regardless of the outcome. My personal quiet time with the Lord and quality time with my family became treasures like never before.

God taught me to be dependent upon His strength and grace during my weakness. How can the gold be purified without the furnace? We all want to stay on the mountaintop, but this vital lesson can only be experienced in the valley. Your pain can be your greatest teacher. It can certainly give you an eternal perspective. Maybe the timing wasn't so bad after all. I enjoyed the sweet fellowship of my wife with fresh eyes opened by gratitude. And a few months later, I entered that new building knowing it was His strength, not mine, that would give me the supernatural power I needed to shepherd His Church.

My trial only lasted a few months, but the one our next endurance runner encountered lasted half a lifetime. At the tender age of seventeen, Joseph was betrayed by his jealous brothers for disclosing a vision God gave him. His brothers, in an act of unspeakable cruelty, sold him as a slave to foreigners who took him in chains to a distant land, thrusting him into a vastly different culture that was void of God's Word and fellowship. As if this was not enough injustice to endure, Joseph was then falsely accused of rape and sentenced to jail for thirteen long, discouraging years. Yet, in the face of trial after trial, Joseph remained faithful to the Lord, believing in His goodness and redeeming power.

It may surprise you to find out that the author of Hebrews picked none of these mighty acts of faith to secure Joseph's place among the great endurance runners of chapter eleven. It was his endurance to cross the finish line that was his ultimate act of faith.

"By faith Joseph, at the end of his life, made mention of the exodus of the Israelites and gave directions concerning his bones" (Hebrews 11:22).

Joseph didn't just hold on to the dreams God personally gave him as a teenager. He believed God would eventually fulfill the promise given to his great-grandfather, Abraham. Joseph had faith that one day his descendants would enter the Promised Land and carry his bones with them. Sometimes, the path to the Promised Land is through a desert. Though he was elevated to the second greatest position of power and influence in all Egypt, he chose the future blessing God promised him over present pleasures. Joseph's faith was not determined by what he saw but by what he trusted God to fulfill. This simple act of faith is more important than all the acts of his trial-filled life. His faith was strong because the Lord already delivered him from the pit and prison. What matters most is that he remained faithful to the end. Faith is the evidence of things not seen, and Joseph's faith went beyond the grave.[1]

Joseph remained faithful to God, but even this did not spare him from trials. Many ask how a good God could allow the innocent to suffer. Some say suffering is a part of life and there is no escape. Others say it is punishment. Prosperity preachers claim that if you suffer trials, you're not receiving God's favor by faith. These skewed views are wrong. By proclaiming them, certain people are preaching a different Gospel than the one Jesus gave us. It's just not biblical.

Jesus promises, "In this world you will have trials."[2] Jesus suffered. Did He never escape His suffering? Was He being punished for sin? Absolutely not. He was raised from the dead after living a perfect, sinless life and suffering for our sake. And now He sits at the right hand of the Father in glory. Many say they want to be like Jesus, but do they understand what it takes? Like our Savior, if we want to look more like Him and "share in His glory," we must "follow in His steps," pick up our cross, and follow Him.[3] Where else can you pick up your cross but here in this life? God doesn't just intend to glorify you for all eternity. He desires to use your suffering right here on Earth for a mighty Kingdom purpose. It was true for Joseph, it was true for me, and it's also true for you.

You can't always control what happens to you, but you can control your response. Walk in humility knowing God is God and you are not. Perspective is crucial. Having a plan of action and deciding to endure before the race are essential keys to keeping your faith during your trials. Apply these Biblical principles when life knocks you down and watch how God's promises will not return empty because He is faithful to complete the good work He has begun in you.[4]

TRUST

Joseph retained a positive attitude and never once abandoned his trust in the Lord. Through God's power, you can do the same. When things hit the fan, the knee-jerk reaction is to worry and complain, just as my "friend" Google tempted me to do. Reacting this way will only keep you down and prevent you from moving forward in your race. Jesus tells us not to worry because not only will it hurt you, it will also send a message to those who are watching you. Do you really believe God is in control? Courage follows fear and trust follows trials. Proverbs 24:10 says, "If you faint in the day of adversity, your strength is small." But the power is not your own. It comes from a brokenness only produced in this fallen world by suffering. Remember what 2 Corinthians 12:9 says: "My power is made perfect in weakness." For the believer, strength follows submission.

So, when things don't go your way, lean on the Lord and know the most important quality you can possess is a positive attitude. Corrie Ten Boom says, reminiscing about her trial in Germany during WWI, "When a train goes through a dark tunnel, you don't throw away the ticket and jump off. You sit still and trust the engineer." You can't always choose when or what kind of trouble happens to you, but you can choose your attitude. Peace is not the absence of trials but the presence of God. Like

Jesus, choose to look ahead to the joy set before you in eternity and find joy in the suffering.[5] Choose to trust in Jesus.

TEACHABLE

Maybe pride caused Joseph to share the vision God gave him too early. But imagine the humility that developed in his life through those trials. God's desire was not to crush Joseph under unbearable suffering. It was to develop the necessary character to fulfill his calling and future leadership role in Egypt. Joseph had to humbly submit himself, and by doing so the Lord used him to save many, including saving his family from a seven-year drought. But long before Joseph was entrusted to live in the palace, he spent years in prison. That tiny room had a low ceiling and stone walls. Prisoners were given just enough bread and water to survive because death would have been a reward. What if Joseph became bitter? I don't deserve this. It's not fair. I quit. He submitted to God and learned obedience through suffering.

God uses pressure, heat, and time to create diamonds in both rocks and people. Great souls are forged through struggles, storms, and suffering. Be patient during the process. The trial you face now will prepare you for bigger trials you'll overcome in the future. See these trials as an opportunity for growth and maturation. Good parents discipline their children to help in the maturity process. God does the same. But don't waste the trials. Remember, "for the moment all discipline seems painful rather than pleasant, but later it yields the peaceful fruit of righteousness to those who have been trained by it."[6] Be trained by them. Be teachable and don't worry or complain. God will not allow you to face a trial He hasn't given you the grace to overcome. When you are going through your trial, don't harden your heart. Instead, ask, "What can I take away from this to help me grow?"

TRIUMPH

Joseph may have thought he was victorious when God enabled him to interpret the cup bearer's dream, asking the cup bearer to mention him to Pharaoh so that he could be released from prison. But days turned to weeks, weeks turned to months, and months turned to years. It took two long years for Joseph to finally enjoy the triumph he'd thought was coming sooner. God's delays are not denials. The Lord often delays His help until the last moment. It was so with Abraham, who held a knife in his hand and prepared to offer Isaac while his son was bound on an altar. It was so with Moses at the Red Sea. It was so with the disciples in a boat during a storm when they thought death was imminent. It was so with Peter in prison. It was so with Martha who thought it was too late when her brother Lazarus died. It was so with Jesus on the cross and in the grave before His resurrection. It was with me during the dark nights and weeks I waited for biopsy results. And it will be with you. The apostle writes in Hebrews 10:38, "My righteous one shall live by faith, and if he shrinks back, My soul has no pleasure in him." By God's power you will overcome your trial. If you quit early through fear, God will have no pleasure in you.

When traveling through your trial to get to your paradise, you need your own "triumph." Just like the true victory residing in my spiritual victory, the same is true for you. Triumph is not a what but a Who. Jesus promises in John 16:33 (NLT), "I have told you all this so that you may have peace in me. Here on earth you will have many trials and sorrows. But take heart, because I have overcome the world." Your Triumph is Jesus. Have faith that the bad things will eventually be in the past. The outcome of your trial may not end in the victory you initially hoped for. But if you see Jesus as your Triumph and place your trust in the Lord instead of in surgeries or biopsies, you will experience sweet victory and the supernatural peace to help you endure.

This kind of peace can't be found in a bottle. There are a few things in life that can numb the pain, but only Jesus can give you a peace that will overflow beyond your pain, that will give you "wings like eagles" to renew your strength and soar over every trial.[7] This is the peace that passes beyond all understanding.[8] Jesus will never allow you to face a trial without the grace necessary to overcome it.[9]

TESTIMONY

Concerning the burial of his bones, Joseph testifying to his faith in God's promise to Abraham that his people would one day enter the Promised Land didn't just minister to his family while he lay on his deathbed. He also ministered to the Hebrews who would one day, centuries later, carry his bones across the Jordan and now, millennia later, testify to the faithfulness of God's promises to all people.

What if God isn't testing you because He's mad at you. What if He wants to use you to reveal Jesus to the world? I wouldn't say it was easy or comfortable to share my tumor experience in all its detail, but how else can I testify to the full grace and glory of our Lord Jesus Christ? Don't be afraid to testify. As Paul did, boast in nothing else but your weaknesses and the cross of Christ.[10] Your weaknesses show your need for a savior and boasting in the cross shows who your Savior is.

Missionary E. Stanley Jones tells a story from the turn of the century. A bright, vivacious, European college student, who became a teacher, lived in the city of Rangoon in Burma. Life seemed to hold beautiful promise for her. But before her sun rose to its summit, it suddenly became a dark cloud. She contracted leprosy. The terminal disease would eventually cause parts of her body to die.

She tried to hide the dreadful illness but could not. She left the country for treatment and came back free of symptoms. She began teaching again, but the disease returned. She thought if she went back for treatment, it would be all over. She tried to deny the fact she had it, but to no avail.

One day she deliberately left her classroom and walked the two miles to the leper asylum. She hesitated a long time before the gates, knowing if they closed on her this time, they wouldn't open for her again. She cried out to God and entered. Blocked from teaching on the outside, she focused her attention on teaching the lepers. She even arranged a choir and taught them how to sing. In doing so, her own heart became radiant as she too sang a new song. The song of triumph was passed on from generation to generation just like the faith of Joseph.[11]

Your trial becomes your testimony. People around you are more interested when you allow them to journey through your trials, in all their unflattering display, with you. Your vulnerability allows them to be vulnerable, enabling you to "bear one another's burdens, and so fulfill the law of Christ."[12] One of the most powerful things you can say to a suffering friend is "Me too." Ask God to bring people into your life who face the same trial you did. He desires you to be a pain partner. They need to know they are not alone, and God will be glorified when you help them trust. Embrace the real purpose of your pain. Don't let the trial be in vain. God wastes nothing. You shouldn't either. Instead, use your trial as a strength for God's witness. From your secret place, build an altar. Confess you are facing a giant. Dig deep and trust in the Lord. Watch your trial be the catalyst to launch you into ministry. What God does in you, He does through you. Your story will become your ministry. Your mess will become your message. In every dark moment, hold on to the promise in Galatians 6:9: "And let us not grow weary of doing good, for in due season we will reap, if we do not give up."

9

BE BRAVE

JOCHEBED

Everything you want is on the other side of fear.

JACK CANFIELD

THE POWERLINE DESCENT IS FAST, ROCKY, THREADED WITH deep ruts, and sketchy at best. Once an old jeep road and now a jostling bike trail, the rough terrain cuts beneath an old power line. But the thing about those old lines is they just go straight down the mountain—and I mean straight down. With a heart-stopping elevation loss of 1,300 feet over 3.4 miles at a 7.3 percent average grade, it's one mean sucker. And it was my biggest fear in the Leadville Trail one-hundred-mile, mountain-bike race. This descent has a nasty reputation of ripping apart tire sidewalls and instigating massive crashes. The only way to finish was for courage to conquer my white-knuckle fear.

The fear I felt was real, but I couldn't let it prevent me from finishing the race. It shouldn't have a negative impact on your race for Christ. As 1 Timothy 1:7 says, "for God has not given us a spirit of fear, but of power and love and of a sound mind." God is the only One you should fear. All other fear is not from the Lord, and it will control you and steal your ability to keep your eyes on the prize. Only by submitting yourself to God and resisting the devil will fear be banished. What do you fear most?

The one universal fear and arguably the most powerful of all is the fear of death. Another common fear is the fear of failure. This fear will keep you stagnant, preventing spiritual growth and keeping you from stepping out in faith. Another fear is the self-fulling prophecy keeping you from trying: the fear of never making a difference. And what about questioning the security you have in God's love for you, which is swallowing your joy and peace? The fear of rejection is keeping you from intimate relationships and taking away your ability to "love God with your whole heart." It's keeping you from belonging to a church family or a small group of friends.

What if they don't like me? What if they hurt me like before? What if it leads to divorce again?

If you allow your hurt and fear to keep everyone at arm's length, the walls you think protect you are in fact the walls of a self-constructed prison cell of solitary confinement. Yes, all these fears are very real and too powerful to overcome on your own. But even though this is "impossible with man, all things are possible with God." Only by surrendering your fears to God will you overcome and fulfill God's purpose for your life.

The next endurance runner listed in Hebrews 11 was tempted to give in to the fear of others. When indulged, this fear can bring about devastating consequences. It puts your focus on what others will think of you, say about you, or do to you. You trade blessed assurance for shaky ground, and ultimately you don't trust God, His power, or His love for you. You fear man more than God. But this endurance runner did not allow fear to prevent her from doing what she knew God wanted her to do.

The number of the children of Israel had grown so much that the pharaoh of Egypt feared an insurrection from the people he enslaved. This wicked pharaoh decreed that Hebrew midwives must kill every male child at birth by throwing them into the Nile River. The consequence of disobeying this horrifying command was certain death.

"By faith Moses, when he was born, was hidden for three months by his parents, because they saw that the child was beautiful, and they were not afraid of the king's edict."[1]

The story of Jochebed, the mother of Moses, is one of bravery. But where does this kind of astonishing bravery come from? How can you find it? How do you live a life of bravery as Jochebed did? Bravery is defined as the courage to endure danger without showing fear. Showing, not feeling. Bravery is a response to fear. We all face it; it is a consequence of the Fall. You can either give in to the temptation, or you can go to the only One who will give you this unshakable courage.

The consistent call of God is "do not fear" and "be strong and courageous." This message is found 119 times in Scripture! "Be strong and courageous. Do not be frightened, and do not be dismayed, for the Lord your God is with you wherever you go" (Joshua 1:9). Why does God say this to us over and over again? Because He knows fear is one of our biggest obstacles, and He wants to encourage us to remember that He is the almighty God of the universe and that He has us in His most capable hands. Just as a father would come to his child's room in the middle of the night and gather him or her in his strong arms after a terrifying nightmare, God desires to do the same for you.

Don't try to fight fear on your own. No matter how frightening your situation is, there is every reason to be brave. If you walk in obedience and love, you can trust that God will give you all the courage you need. He will not just be the source, He will be with you. "Even though I walk through the valley of the shadow of death, I will fear no evil, for You are with me" (Psalm 23:4).

I recently came across a video recording of my son Bryce flying down our steep driveway on his bike when he was just four years old. As he plummeted down the hill, he yelled out confidently, "I closed my eyes!" I showed this video to Bryce, and he responded by asking, "Who is that little boy?"

I said, "That boy is you!"

He couldn't believe it because now, at the age of eleven, he walks his bike down the driveway. Why? I'm sure I have a good idea of the root cause. A few years ago, he suffered a bad accident at a bike park in Colorado, falling off a ramp and tumbling down five feet.

After watching the video together again, I reminded him of Ephesians 6:10, the life verse God gave him a few years earlier when his poppy died, "...Finally, be strong in the Lord and in the strength of His might." I looked him in the eyes and said, "Son, there's still that same bravery inside of you." Bryce must have trusted what I told him was the truth because he immediately went to the garage and pulled out his mountain bike. I'll never forget the determined look on his face as he flew down the driveway. He was alive and set free! By God's power as the author and finisher of his faith, Bryce trusted what the Lord spoke over him in his life verse, and it empowered him to overcome his fear.

When you lack what it takes to conquer fear, look for help but remember where your true help comes from. Courage is a word derived from the French word "coeur," meaning "heart." Only by opening the throne of your heart for God to be King will you fear Him above all others and find the courage to overcome. J. R. R. Tolkien writes, "Take courage, Lord of the Mark; for better help you will not find."[2] This "better" help comes from the Lord. Discover in Jochebed the key to overcome your greatest fear.

To help you remember how to conquer through Jesus, use this acronym when you're in those moments of fear and need courage: be B.R.A.V.E. I pray this will help you as you face the fears God will enable you to overcome.

BELIEVE THE PROMISE OF GOD

When Jochebed saw her handsome baby boy, she remembered what she heard from God. The whole point of Hebrews 11 focuses on enduring faith. Faith comes from hearing and hope rests on believing what is heard from God. It must be inferred that Jochebed heard from the Lord what would happen and what she needed to do to save her child. The Lord must have revealed to her that her child was to be the promised deliverer and gave her a vision of what he would look like.

The first step in overcoming your fear is remembering God's promises. Trust in His character and trust in His promises. He promises to always be with you so that you are never alone. He promises to strengthen you when you feel weak. "The Lord is my light and my salvation; Whom shall I fear? The Lord is the stronghold of my life; of whom shall I be afraid?" (Psalms 27:1).

Do you want to see His promise fulfilled? You must overcome your fear through Christ. Fear is a result of focusing on the bad and forgetting what God has promised. God keeps His promises. When you forget His promises, you become afraid.

REFLECT ON GOD'S BLESSINGS

Imagine the sweet three months when Jochebed nursed her precious baby. All other baby boys were murdered by the pharaoh. She was grateful to hold a survivor with a purpose in her arms. "Behold, children are a heritage from the Lord, the fruit of the womb a reward" (Psalm 127:3).

When fear tries to creep in, list God's blessings. Remember what He's already done in your life. Thank God for every one of them. A grateful heart protects your mind from being afraid, and the reminder of His faithfulness and power will make your current problem seem small in comparison to His power. Remember, the Lord doesn't leave you alone in those moments. In fact, His Word promises in 1 Corinthians 10:13 that in every temptation the Lord has already provided a way of escape, so you will be able to endure it. Jesus will conquer through you when you look to Him.

AVOID THE HATERS

Jochebed refused to be intimidated by the cruel command of an evil ruler. Instead, she obeyed the orders from a greater ruler, the King of kings. The fear of the Lord was upon her, and therefore she was not afraid of man.

A fuel for fear is listening to the wrong voices. It wasn't just the voice of an evil ruler threatening her. I imagine Jochebed had neighbors and family members who were more concerned about her life than her baby's survival. Hiding the baby meant certain death. If you listen to the haters, they will bring you down. They will draw you away from the Lord and your only hope to conquer. Negative people tell you every reason why you will fail or why it's not worth the risk. They delight in presenting the worst possible scenario as fact. This makes them feel important and like they are your savior rather than Christ. Listening to their words will only feed your fears.

Never be afraid of what others in the world might think of or say about you. Fear God or man, you can't do both. If you fear God, you will never fear man. The Lord says in Matthew 10:28, "And do not fear those who kill the body but cannot kill the soul. Rather fear him who can destroy both soul and body in hell."

May you possess the same courageous faith from Jesus, the faith which overcomes all fear of man. I imagine the author of Hebrews thought of Jochebed when later writing in Hebrews 13:6, "So we can confidently say, 'The Lord is my helper; I will not fear; what can man do to me?'" Silence the haters in your life.

VISUALIZE THE WAY TO VICTORY

Would Jochebed look over her shoulder or trust God to find a better future? Had she lacked faith, Jochebed would have conceded to fear and the pharaoh's command. Instead, she fixed her eyes on the Lord. The reward in saving her son from the pharaoh's edict was not just the survival of an infant but the survival of a nation. This dangerous road was secure because she trusted God and knew it was right in His eyes.

Fear is a choice of what you visualize. Who do you look to for your salvation? Focusing on the wrong things will keep you from moving forward in your race and will most certainly keep you from victory. What you focus on will determine your future. If you focus on all the negative, fear-driven things in life, know your race will end in failure. Your skewed focus is what makes you afraid. Fear happens when you visualize the bad. It's a self-fulfilling prophecy. The more you look for the bad things in life, the more you'll find them and the more you'll replay those possible, fear-driven outcomes in your mind, which will only make your fear grow. Like a fog, fear brings confusion and clouds your vision. It exaggerates the bad in your mind. If you don't choose to focus on the right things—on the promises of God to be your shield, your protection, your guide—you'll give in to your fears and the battle will already be lost.

Overcoming fear requires you to change what you visualize. It's your choice. Set your mind on things above as Colossians 3:2 commands. You can be delivered from fear once and for all when you focus on victory in Jesus. That's what faith does. Faith focuses on God's provision instead of the problems. Faith focuses on God's opportunity instead of the obstacles. Faith focuses on Christ instead of the crowd. There was enormous pressure on Jochebed to follow the crowd, but she knew she had a higher purpose—pleasing God. Change your focus. Choose to please

God instead of attempting to please the crowd. You will never please everybody all the time. Run to please God.

What does God want you to dwell on? Ask Him to confirm it through Scripture and wise advice from trusted friends. Philippians 4:8 says, "Finally, brothers, whatever is true, whatever is honorable, whatever is just, whatever is pure, whatever is lovely, whatever is commendable, if there is any excellence, if there is anything worthy of praise, think about these things."

God's plan for you is bigger than your problems. Get a hold of God's vision and never let go. Don't allow yourself to get distracted by the negative voices. He desires to use you for His perfect purpose. He desires to bless you. Focus on your God, not your problems. Focusing on your problems leads to fear *every* time, but focusing on the Lord will lead to faith. God is on your side. He is for you. By faith, worship the Lord even in the midst of those negative voices pulling at you. Worship is praising God. It puts your focus on Him and His promised victory instead of on your fears.

EXECUTE FAITH

It's not enough to simply believe because "even the demons believe."[3] Instead, you must execute faith and act because "faith without works is dead." That's what faith does. It was "by faith" Jochebed acted and put her actions where her heart was. She loved Moses enough to put her own life on the line to hide him for three months. But all too soon the time came when it was no longer possible to keep him to herself. As if her courage to defy the pharaoh's orders was not brave enough, she later let him go and literally placed him in the hands of God. She saved her son's life again by making a wooden chest of bulrushes. It was watertight with pitch to protect Moses, but what about crocodiles? Undertows? Jochebed walked out of her hiding at the exact time He who ordered it all knew pharaoh's daughter would be walking. Jochebed committed her son to the waters of the same river many other babies were drowned in. Her faith in the only One she knew could truly deliver her son saved his life and later saved a nation.

Perhaps taking a deep breath and wiping tears from her cheeks, she kissed him one last time and released the chest to float in the Nile while Miriam, her daughter, kept watch over it from a distance. But God was never distant from him. He was the only One who could save Moses now. And then, another miracle occurred. Moses was discovered by the pharaoh's daughter, Bithia, who came to the river to swim. God touched her heart, caused favor, and gave Bithia compassion. Not only did she save Moses and draw him from the river, she also decided to adopt him. Imagine letting go of your child with no guarantee of his safety. Jochebed executed great faith when she placed her trust in God to care for Moses, and the Lord didn't fail her. Be inspired by her faith that conquered her fear. Faith is the spiritual grace to help you act in the middle of terror. It's a choice. When you choose faith instead of fear, you'll receive your reward. According to Jewish legend, Jochebed is buried in the Tomb of the Matriarchs, in Tiberias. She was honored and remembered because of her faith and love and, more importantly, because God would eventually use her son to deliver a nation from its oppressors.

It is your choice. Submit yourself to God and no longer allow fear to paralyze you, to prevent you from carrying out God's purpose for your life. Trust in the Lord. Love Him and others enough to act. 1 John 4:18 says, "There is no fear in love, but perfect love casts out fear." When you experience God's love, it drives out your fears and takes care of every imaginable problem. What's the next step of faith God is calling you to take? Confess and repent of a sin? Get baptized in water? Surrender whatever it is to the Lord. Ask a friend how you can pray for him or her. Share your story and how God has delivered you through faith with a friend. Start tithing. Offer to help a co-worker. Invite a neighbor over for dinner. Start volunteering at your church or in your community. Read your Bible this week. Do something. Keep taking another step.

God will bless your obedience. You'll discover His plan for your life is wonderful and far better than anything you could ever imagine. "What no eye has seen, nor ear heard, nor the heart of man imagined, what God has prepared for those who love Him." You'll discover His blessing on your finances when you manage His resources well. You'll see your friends surrender their lives to Jesus. Obey, plant, and water, and God will bring the increase.

Acting in faith is always worth it. It was worth it for God. John 3:16 says, "For God so loved the world, that He gave his only Son, that whoever believes in Him should not perish but have eternal life." Fear didn't keep Mary from keeping Jesus safe when King Herod made a similar command to murder all male babies. Fear didn't keep Jesus from resisting the devil who tried to tempt Him. Fear didn't keep Jesus from laying down His life to be crucified on a cross. The enemy thought he won when Jesus died on a cross, but ultimately God was victorious through His son's resurrection and obedience to the will of His Father. "Not my will, but Yours be done." He saved you from your sin. He rescued you from hell. You were worth it.

A story is told by missionary E. Stanley Jones. Several years ago, a young lady who was seventeen years old disobeyed her parents and went to a party. She was raised in a God-fearing home, but she compromised her values. She drank too much and lost her virginity to a man she barely knew. Shame and fear kept her from going back home. She moved in with the wrong kind of friends. She numbed her pain with more drinking and more sex. Soon she started financially supporting herself by selling her body. Her parents were devastated. They prayed constantly for God to save their daughter. When they discovered she had become a prostitute, they traveled to every community in their state. Into every brothel, they brought a photograph of their daughter when she was fifteen. They questioned everyone who may have seen their girl. They wrote two words on her picture: COME HOME. After a few months, she saw the picture of her younger self on the mantle of a fireplace. It reminded her of the innocence she lost, and the handwriting reminded her of the love she was missing. She ran out the door and returned home.

Faith subdues fears and produces bravery. Be encouraged. Keep doing what's right even if you don't see immediate results. Galatians 6:9 says, "And let us not grow weary of doing good, for in due season we will reap, if we do not give up." Don't quit just before your harvest.

10

KNOW WHO YOU ARE

MOSES

Find your identity outside of
what you do and how you look.

ALL ODDS FAVORED RUNNER ERIC LIDDELL TO WIN HIS BEST event, the one-hundred-meter dash, in the 1924 Olympics. Unfortunately, the race took place on a Sunday. Silencing the voices of friends, teaammates, and his country that encouraged him to participate, Eric would not compromise his conviction. He resisted the pressures and temptation to yield and instead obeyed God's command to rest on the Sabbath. The movie *Chariots of Fire* reveals he still won gold in the 400-meter race—an event he didn't even train for. Liddell understood his identity was not found on the track but as a child of God.

A year later, Lindell was sent to China as a missionary. He was arrested and incarcerated in a concentration camp. A fellow prisoner who watched him die said, "What was his secret? Eric unreservedly committed his life to Jesus Christ as his Savior and Lord. That friendship meant everything to him. By the flickering light of a peanut-oil lamp early each morning, he studied the Bible and talked with God an hour every day. As a Christian, Eric's desire was to know God more deeply; and as a missionary, to make Him known more fully." Liddell's reward eclipsed the winning of a gold medal and the suffering of persecution. He is now in heaven rejoicing. Liddell gave up so much to obey the Lord's conviction and then gave his very life. He finished his race.

Insecurity and a lack of identity will keep you from moving forward in your race.

The next endurance runner found in Hebrews 11 had a lot riding on him. The promise of deliverance to generations of Israelites would come down to a choice, a choice Moses made over and over again, a choice that had everything to do with identity.

By faith Moses, when he was grown up, refused to be called the son of pharaoh's daughter, choosing to be mistreated along with the people of God rather than enjoy the fleeting pleasures of sin. "He considered the reproach of Christ greater wealth than the treasures of Egypt because he was looking to the reward" (Hebrews 11:24–26).

Moses discovered *who you are* is more important than what you do. Like Liddell, Moses had to silence the voices telling him to live by a false identity. His example will help you discover your true identity and how to silence the negative voices in your own life.

Moses was raised by the pharaoh's daughter like he was her own son. It was the only life he knew. When Moses turned forty, he faced a pivotal moment. He had the opportunity to remain part of the royal family, but he must have heard from God not to accept it. This is the reason it took faith. Since faith comes from hearing, Moses clearly heard from God. But he also believed what

God said about him rather than his adoptive family. This was the only reason it must have been so fulfilling for him to turn his back on the prestige and riches for a more difficult assignment. This faith required him to silence the three voices you will be tempted to listen to.

THE VOICE OF YOURSELF

When God called Moses to be His man to tell the pharaoh to release the Israelites from captivity, Moses quickly came up with an excuse: Choose someone else because I stutter. Moses doubted himself. He believed he wasn't qualified. But Scripture shows a pattern of God selecting nobodies and making them somebodies. Have you ever doubted yourself? I know I have.

When God called me to preach, I quickly explained to God why my introverted, shy nature caused me terror at the thought of public speaking. I reminded him of the proof when I got a D in speech class. Excuses to God are like armpits; they all stink. God doesn't call the qualified. He qualifies the called. The way to overcome insecurity is to have real, unshakable faith in the Lord and what He says about you. You will always feel insecure or inadequate if you trust in yourself or listen to the other voices in your life.

Perhaps someone made fun of Moses when he was growing up in the palace. Perhaps even his wife or father-in-law did. We all carry wounds from words spoken over us. And because these people have sewn words into our lives, we tend to say them back to ourselves and repeat them over our lives. You must not allow them to color your decisions and shape your identity. Be careful about how you speak to yourself. Words are free. They are easily spent. But as Proverbs 18:21 says, “Death and life are in the power of the tongue.” God did not create us for death but for life. Though you cannot forget hurtful words, forgive the ones who spoke them over you. Only then will you be able to silence all the voices contrary to the nature of God and what His words say about you. Silence all the voices that say your identity must be in how you look or what you do.

THE VOICE OF A “POPULAR” IDENTITY

Moses knew only one culture. He grew up speaking and dressing like the rest of the Egyptians. It shaped him in every way. It must have been daunting for him to leave the only world he knew for another.

My world changed in the fifth grade when our family moved from Texas to New Hampshire. New Englanders have a certain way of saying things. They drop the “r’s” from their vocabulary. If something is difficult, it’s “wicked hahd.” Imagine being invited to a birthday “pahty.” I struggled. I was an insecure, shy kid who desperately wanted to fit in.

The only thing I had going for me was the perception that everyone from Texas is a cowboy. My elementary school classmates were already intrigued by my southern accent. They had never seen a “real” cowboy in person before. I didn’t own boots, listen to country music, or ride a horse, but I understood that it would be a giant, social setback if I denied being one.

After the third day of school, I found an empty can of Copenhagen tobacco on my street and put it in my back pocket because that's what cowboys did, right? They chewed tobacco. It must have worked because I'll never forget the moment Christine Palmer walked up to me in the middle of class. She told me, "I've always wanted to kiss a cowboy." I felt like Doc Holliday in the movie *Tombstone*. On the outside I was speechless, but on the inside I was her "huckleberry." Excitement, shock, and maybe even a little fear zinged through me at her boldness. I told her I was her man, and right there, in front of everyone, she laid one on me. It was my first kiss. I went from being a cowboy to king of the entire fifth grade. It was arguably a "top-ten" moment in my life.

Have you tried to become someone you're not? God never intended you to be someone else. He wants you to be you. Don't look for purpose and identity in the wrong places. The enticing voice of choosing a different, "more popular" identity is loud and everywhere. The voices that say you must be skinny, sexy, and smart are intended to conform you to a cultural ideal. It's tempting but it's dangerous. Not only are you lying to yourself and others, you are also robbing God of the opportunity to bless others through the person He made, called, and always needed you to be. You don't have to look a certain way to be successful. You don't need a certain degree to make "x" amount of money. The Bible says, "Do not be conformed to this world, but be transformed by the renewal of your mind" (Romans 12:2).

THE VOICE OF OTHERS

Imagine the heart of the only mother Moses ever knew, the one who rescued him from the river. She must have begged

Moses not to leave. Her intentions were good, but her voice was distracting Moses from God's calling. It would cause him to second-guess the voice of God.

You remember being told as a child "sticks and stones may break my bones, but words will never hurt me." Whoever told you this was full of it. Words are powerful, but they don't have to define you. During your formative years, the voices of your friends, enemies, teachers, bosses, family members, and even pastors shaped the thoughts you now have about yourself. You may never forget their words, but you can choose to forgive them. God will bring healing and you can always discover a kernel of truth in the worst criticism.

Social media makes this choice even more difficult. When I was young, all I had to fight was the feeling of unpopularity. I was five foot one as a freshman in high school. Although mom said I was a "late bloomer," my class mates had other, less friendly words to describe my vertically challenged condition. Although I grew to six feet, I became "follicly" challenged. If I had a dime for every bald joke I heard—I'd be a very rich man. Today, a lack of "followers" or "friends" makes the same statement. Sending out a tweet is not the way to make yourself feel validated. Constantly checking for "likes" will cement a bad habit of finding worth in the wrong voices.

As Moses did, silence the voices and find your true, eternal identity in Jesus and repeat to yourself what He says about you.

CHOOSE YOUR TRUE IDENTITY

I grew up not very happy with how many freckles God placed on me. I wanted to punch every kid in the throat who called me

"Freckle Face" at recess. Way too many moments were wasted on wishing I had a clear, tanned face. My daughter revealed to me freckles are the latest trend. People are paying money to get them tattooed. Are you serious?

The voice of God must be stronger than the voices of others. By faith, Moses walked out of the palace and into the wilderness. He chose to identify with his mistreated Israelites instead of with the royalty of Egypt. By faith, you must hear from God about your own identity. Your identity is who you are in Christ, not what you do. Change your perspective on yourself. If identity is in what you do, you'll rob God of His glory for any success. And because you are creating your own identity, you'll be wrecked when you fail because you placed the burden on yourself instead of on God. You don't work for your identity, you work from your identity.

What if you were happy with the way God made you? What if the source of your identity and self-worth was not how you looked? God created you to be you. View yourself the way God views you. Love yourself the way God loves you. Find your value and identity in Him alone. Who you are in Christ will change the way you think and act. You will be known by your choices just like Moses and Eric Liddell. Choose your identity based on the Word of God. Trust in the Lord that He knew exactly what He was doing when He created you. You never know. The little details you don't like today can be what you will be grateful for tomorrow.

What does God say about you?

"So God created man in His own image, in the image of God He created him; male and female He created them" (Genesis 1:27). You are created by God with intrinsic value no one can take away. Not a single sparrow can fall to the ground without your Father knowing it. Don't be afraid! You are more valuable to God than a whole flock of sparrows.

"For you formed my inward parts; you knitted me together in my mother's womb. I praise you, for I am fearfully and wonderfully made" (Psalm 139:13–14). You mattered to God while He formed you in your mother's womb. No one else has your fingerprint. God gave you a unique personality, important spiritual gifts, and abilities for a great purpose. Remind yourself of this: I must live in God's grace. I must focus on the TRUTH. And when I do, I get to tell my unique story.

"God shows his love for us in that while we were still sinners, Christ died for us" (Romans 5:8). If it was all taken away, would you still trust that Jesus loves you? The cross is proof of His love for you no matter what.

"But you are a chosen race, a royal priesthood, a holy nation, a people for His own possession, that you may proclaim the excellencies of Him who called you out of darkness into His marvelous light" (1 Peter 2:9). God has chosen you and will anoint you to tell others the good news of Jesus.

"Therefore, if anyone is in Christ, he is a new creation. The old has passed away; behold, the new has come" (2 Corinthians 5:17). Don't allow the shame of your past to influence your identity. When people see how far God has brought you, they will want what you have and believe change is possible for them through Jesus. They will know through your example that when you surrender your life to Jesus as Savior and Lord, you are new.

"But to all who did receive Him, who believed in His name, He gave the right to become children of God" (John 1:12). You are not an orphan. You are His son. You are His daughter. You are part of the family of God, so you will never be alone. I'm a pastor. It's what I do, but it's not who I am. When your identity is found solely in being a child of God, your life will never be shaken. Trust the way God sees you; He sees you as His child. Who you are in Christ will change the way you think and act.

Jesus tells a story of a man who found a treasure while walking through a field. Once he discovered the value of the land, he sold everything to purchase the field. Nothing was off limits because the treasure was more valuable. Jesus is your treasure. Consider Him to be most valuable. You are created and loved by the One who is most valuable.

Moses knew Who his true treasure was. He realized his purpose would not be found in leading the kingdom of Egypt but in leading the people of God. His purpose was found in becoming a leader in the Kingdom of heaven. He regarded the "reproach of Christ" as greater wealth than the treasures of Egypt. Just as Jesus left the comfort of heaven to rescue His lost children, God honored the faith of Moses by allowing him to lead a ragamuffin group of Israelites out of Egypt. With an army chasing them from behind and facing the impossible Red Sea in front, Moses courageously obeyed God's voice to move forward. By faith, Moses received the Ten Commandments. You must have real faith in God, or you will not be able to go where He wants your faith to take you.

Jesus is in you. You have a God-created strength in you. Find great peace in being yourself. Don't fight it. Don't wrap your identity in what you do. It's who you are in Christ. Who you are in Jesus will overcome your emotions of feeling unqualified and inadequate. Be confident in this truth. It's not what you do, but who you are in Christ.

11

ALL IN

RAHAB

Life is either a daring adventure or nothing.

Helen Keller

One spring break I surprised my family with the idea to take a spontaneous road trip to Austin. I woke our three kids at 5:45 a.m. and told them to load their backpacks with clothes and a toothbrush, but I didn't tell them where we were headed. Even Stephanie didn't know the final destination. We drove to downtown San Antonio and arrived at the historic Sunset Station less than an hour later. I thought it would be fun to take a train instead of fighting the morning, rush hour traffic on I-35 on our way to Austin. After dropping my family off at the gate, I circled several times but couldn't find a single open parking space. A nearby event caused the early morning crowd to spill over into the train station's parking lot. What was going on? I had no idea and couldn't find any signs, but I knew the attendees weren't going anywhere any time soon this early in the morning.

Feeling rushed, I turned right out of the parking lot and drove down E Commerce Street then left on Hackberry Street, scouring the sides of the streets for a spot. I didn't find one for eight blocks. I had what I thought was plenty of time to make it back before the train's 7:00 a.m. departure. But I didn't want to chance it, so I took off at a mad sprint.

After running a couple of blocks down Hackberry, I heard hasty footsteps behind me and a lot of huffing and puffing. Since I was downtown and the sun wasn't up yet, the chances were this wouldn't be a favorable encounter. I faced a pivotal decision. Would I surrender to the possible assailant or run like my pants were on fire?

I ran.

When I couldn't hold him off any longer, I looked over my shoulder to prepare myself for the standoff and noticed the strangest thing. The "criminal" wore neon socks and a race bib. And he wasn't alone. A whole pack of people behind him wore matching apparel.

Unless this was some weird new gang, I was in a race. And not in the middle of it, in the lead pack.

Since Van Pay's aren't known for their speed, I was already gassed and in pain from the lactic acid buildup in my blood. But I felt a new shot of adrenaline when I realized something.

I could win. Or at least feel like it!

As if God chose this moment for me as a humorous but fantastic gift, I somehow picked up my pace and passed the lead runners. Who cares if they had already run three miles? I was going to win. I could see the bright floodlights and a glorious finish line only two blocks away. Every ounce of my competitive nature on display, I started swinging my elbows wide in one final desperate attempt. Although two runners passed me, elation filled me all the way down to my soul when I crossed the finish line in "third place" in the annual Run with the Presidents 5K.

Since spectators, runners, and volunteers cheered for me, I couldn't help but feel proud of my "hard-earned" accomplishment. When I mentioned I was only running to catch a train, they wouldn't listen. It was chaos. People swarmed me. A volunteer handed me a towel, water bottle, and a finisher's t-shirt. A photographer raised his camera, signaling if I wanted my photo taken. I checked my watch—sure, I had time. One runner shook my hand to congratulate me because he never saw anyone make the podium while wearing cargo shorts and a windbreaker before. Embracing the absurd but fun situation I'd found myself in, I responded while pumping my chest with my fist, "C'mon, bro, you know it's all about the engine."

Still a little out of breath and carrying my "finisher's" gear, I finally made it back to Sunset Station with several minutes to spare. We all had a great, unexpected laugh that morning as I shared the play-by-play of my "accomplishment" in glorious detail.

Why would God choose a random Tuesday morning for such a remarkable finish? Most of the time you choose the race, but on rare occasions God allows the race to choose you.

When you arrive at the fork in the road of life, will you choose to risk it all or play it safe? Giving in to the temptation to stay comfortable will plateau your growth. Those who never step out in faith will eventually settle for an average, boring life.

Don't miss life's greatest adventures. Killer whales are created to swim freely in the big, blue ocean. Only 1 percent of them have collapsed dorsal fins in the wild. However, the majority of killer whales in captivity have a dorsal fin bent over their bodies like a drooping, white flag. It's a sign they've given up. Captivity kills everyone. Garth Stein says, "There is no dishonor in losing the race. There is only dishonor in not racing because you are afraid to lose."[1] There is simply no way you can put forth a half-hearted effort and get great results.

> Cowards die many times before their deaths;
> The valiant never taste of death but once.
> Of all the wonders that I yet have heard,
> It seems to me most strange that men should fear;
> Seeing that death, a necessary end,
> Will come when it will come.[2]

The faith of the next person listed in Hebrews 11 is similar to the previous endurance runners, but in her we find a striking contrast that goes beyond the fact that she's a woman. Esther, the brave, beautiful queen, isn't mentioned. Neither is the kind, loyal Ruth or Deborah, the judge of Israel. In this woman, we see an outsider and a harlot with a sordid past. But God didn't see her failures; he saw her faith. She may not have been a Hebrew, but she believed in the Hebrew God. And that was what mattered in the end.

"By faith Rahab the prostitute did not perish with those who were disobedient, because she had given a friendly welcome to the spies" (Hebrews 11:31).

The Israelites were on the eve of finally entering the Promised Land, so their leader, Joshua, sent two spies to check out the city of Jericho. The Holy Spirit led them to the home of an unlikely, new friend, Rahab. What is the specific attribute of faith this woman possessed that allowed her to be awarded the honor of being named among the great endurance runners of the Bible?

When you encounter one who risked it all for something important, take notice. Rahab understood a key principle to finishing her race. If you take an audacious step of faith regardless of your past, God will give you favor. Learn from Rahab's example how to risk it all and embrace the adventures God brings your way.

DON'T LET YOUR PAST HOLD YOU BACK

Joshua Chamberlain was a teacher from Maine who volunteered to join the Union Army during the Civil War. Because of his education, they made him an officer who would become known for his actions at the Battle of Gettysburg.

Chamberlain's regiment could barely hold their lines at a small, rocky outcropping called Little Round Top. His superiors told him to never give up no matter how many attacks they endured from the Confederate Army. When his men ran out of ammunition and their numbers were running low, Chamberlain ordered them to equip their bayonets. He then surprised everyone by calling for an attack down the hill with a "right-wheel forward" maneuver. His unit on the far right would move first then the rest would follow, giving the appearance of a door swinging shut.

When the Confederates witnessed the brave men charging from the side, they assumed reinforcements had arrived. They were no match. Chamberlain led the charge and ran right up to an officer who surrendered immediately. He laid his sword on the officer's shoulder and said, "You, sir, are my prisoner."[3]

Thirty years later, Chamberlain received a Medal of Honor with this inscription: "Daring heroism and great tenacity in holding his position on the Little Round Top against repeated assaults, and ordering the advance position on the Great Round Top." What would've happened if Joshua Chamberlain had asked, "Who am I to lead this charge? I'm just a teacher." Never let the past hold you back from what God wants to do in your future.

When the spies knocked on Rahab's door to introduce themselves, word got out to the king. Instead of cowering at the news and handing them over, she quickly hid them on her roof. Later that evening she paid them a visit to confess her holy fear of the Almighty God and to declare in faith the Lord was giving the Hebrews this land.

Her confession wasn't easy. It wasn't from a place of security or comfort. Imagine how raw her life as a prostitute was. She may have had money, but she had no respect. No love. She lived only to be used. Maybe she was taken advantage of at a young age or abandoned by her husband. Shame followed her everywhere she went. If she looked back like Lot's wife, her destiny would be like the rest of those in the city. By faith, Rahab surrendered her past, security, and her future. She would not be defined by her past but by her faith. Her faith was a bet on the spies and the God of Israel. Rahab went all in.

> "Now then, please swear to me by the Lord that, as I have dealt kindly with you, you also will deal kindly with my father's house, and give me a sure sign that

> you will save alive my father and mother, my brothers and sisters, and all who belong to them, and deliver our lives from death."
>
> And the men said to her, "Our life for yours even to death! If you do not tell this business of ours, then when the Lord gives us the land we will deal kindly and faithfully with you."
>
> Then she let them down by a rope through the window, for her house was built into the city wall, so that she lived in the wall (Joshua 2:12–15).

God inspired the author of Hebrews to choose Rahab, a prostitute and an outsider with no hope of a future, to remove every excuse you may have if your faith comes up short. God has no favorites.[4] There are no small people or small roles in the Kingdom of God. He is color-blind and doesn't see age, gender, or a shady past as legitimate reasons for keeping you from running your race for a great prize. It's always worth it when you let go of what you feel keeps you safe. What is it in your past you need to surrender?

LOWER THE ROPE OF HOPE

Years ago, while Stephanie and I were in Germany to train student ministry leaders, God gave me a dream one night. I saw a man standing in an old building in great need of help. Immediately, the Lord woke me and I found a place to pray in an office in the home of our host missionary. A few days later, our missionary friend, Al Perna, shared a letter with me from his friend asking for financial help to rescue gypsy children via a Teen Challenge ministry in the city of Prague in the Czech Republic. I asked him if he had a picture of his friend, Viteck. When he showed me one, I wept. This was the face of the man in the dream.

I had to go to him. It took a spontaneous, ten-hour train ride to meet Viteck. He and his wife Lucy welcomed me into their humble apartment and then walked me down the street to a building the government gave them permission to use for ministry. They needed a lot of money to fix the roof, or they wouldn't receive the necessary permit to use it. We prayed for God to make a way.

Stephanie and I decided to sell my duck boat and offer money from savings to help. Our pastor allowed us to share the need with our church family who generously gave $30,000 to fix the roof. My encounter with Viteck left a mark on all of us. After he had sacrificed so much, how could we not do whatever it took to help meet the need?

How often does God design divine appointments only waiting for His children to have the faith to obey when He speaks? Going all in drives the heartbeat of God. Holding back breaks His heart.[5] "And without faith it is impossible to please Him" (Hebrews 11:6).

Rahab never flinched. She welcomed the spies into her home, engaged them in spiritual conversation, made provision for their safety, hid them from danger, and refused to betray them. She extended a red rope from her former sinful trade to save a holy nation. God allowed her mess to become her message. He will do the same for you. Don't lower your head thinking your past must be a secret. God wants to turn your story into your ministry. She risked everything. Why? That's what faith does. "Now faith is the assurance of things hoped for, the conviction of things not seen" (Hebrews 11:1). This isn't a definition of faith but an explanation of how faith works. Evidence is proof. Rahab's evidence is the red rope.

GOD BLESSES AUDACIOUS FAITH

Rahab and her family were spared because she hung a red cord out of her window. When the Israelites stormed the city, they skipped the house with the red cord. Surely it was a nice nod to the red blood on the homes of those spared during the Passover. By the faith of Rahab, God rescued her family, the only family that was spared. That's not even the end of the story, though. Rahab was redeemed from her former life and people, and she became a Jewish princess. She married Salmon, the prince of Judah. And as if that wasn't enough to show the gracious, redeeming love of the Lord, turn to Matthew 1:5 and you'll see her name listed in the lineage of Jesus. How is that for a fairy tale ending?

One year after our youngest child, Bryce, was born, God called us to leave our safe, comfortable jobs as student ministry pastors and start a new church with no promise it would work. Reality hit when our Ford Escape and U-Haul trailer crossed the Texas state line. My baby boy screamed his head off in his car seat, demonstrating how the rest of us felt on the inside. We drained our savings account and maxed out our credit cards. We moved our family of five into *one* of my parents' bedrooms. This move cramped everything, including my love life with Stephanie. But like Rahab, by faith, we wouldn't quit, no matter what was thrown at us.

Every big vision has barriers. Every God-sized dream requires God-sized faith. God doesn't call you to play it safe. Don't make conservative decisions at pivotal moments. Audacious faith is essential for trusting God in every area of your life. Testify with boldness. Give beyond what is expected. You serve a God with unlimited resources and wisdom. Life is too short for small faith. You will be scared, but that's what comes with audacious faith.

Speak and act with courage for our Lord Jesus as those who have before you. You will have an opportunity to make a real difference. Dare to take that step of faith. What would happen if you embraced twenty seconds of insane courage? Go all in, and, I promise you, something good will come out of it.

12

DROP THE DEAD WEIGHT

GIDEON

Healthy trees drop dead leaves.

THE DAMAGE DONE BY THE BEAST WAS EXTENSIVE. IN ITS WAKE, it left mangled landscaping, muddy ditches, and uprooted saplings.

Our church family had moved into our permanent home on eleven beautiful acres of Texas Hill Country in San Antonio. God opened many impossible doors and everything still had that rosy sheen and new car smell. But now, instead of enjoying the gift, we were under attack.

I set up a wild-game camera and reviewed the footage daily to discover our intruder. It was a hog. I'm not talking about a bacon-making, curly-tailed, pink darling; that is a domesticated hog. I'm talking about the product of non-native feral hogs breeding with wild boars for the past century. Opportunistic omnivores, their destructive feeding and wallowing habits cost Texans nearly half a billion dollars in damage annually. Millions of them roam our lands unchecked by natural predators. According to the footage on the camera, our own "Hogzilla" had to be at least 300 pounds with four-inch-long tusks.

It was official. Our children were no longer safe. I had to do something. This sucker was going down!

Since we owned at least ten acres, the county only permitted us to hunt with a bow. I called several friends to meet me on top of the thirty-five-foot-high roof of our church later that evening. The entire day we talked up our big party on the church roof and grandiose vision of killing this dim-witted animal. Our plan was simple: consume copious amounts of beef jerky and Dr. Pepper, create fellowship, wait for dark, kill the invading trespasser, celebrate with a feast, and communicate to our church that all was safe.

We ran into two problems. First, the hog never came. Evidently, he didn't grow to his size by being dumb. He could smell and hear us from several hundred yards away. Second, too many of my hunter friends posted pics on social media, broadcasting our failed attempt to hunt the beast. Uncommitted parishioners, as I would call them, made fun of their pastor by cheering for Hogzilla to live another day. My pride was at stake here. Pastor verses Hogzilla. Who would win?

The next evening, we reduced our numbers and allowed no food and trimmed the squad to a father-son hunting team with my good buddy Micah and his boy. Several hours passed before our first real glimpse of the beast. As he approached, foraging in the moonlit clearing, we aimed our bows and, barely breathing with our hearts pumping in anticipation, we waited for the opportune moment. Then, as if he had a sixth sense, something told Hogzilla to pause. He looked up at us, grunted, and ran off.

We stayed up on that roof all night, waiting for another chance that never came.

Hogzilla–2, Pastor–0.

I researched, ramped up my archery skills, and stalked my worthy adversary every night. I logged sixty-five hours of hunting in one week. Regrettably, I even talked my wife into spending our date night on the church roof. She wasn't allowed to talk. Not my best move. I was losing sleep and it exacted a heavy toll on my marriage, family, and ministry. Worse yet, the growing number of hecklers incessantly harassed me. If Hogzilla continued to be victorious, I would be unfit to protect the flock of God. I couldn't give up.

Since I wasn't seeing my kids much, one night during the second week, I invited my daughter Emma to join us. Adding anyone new to our compact, seasoned hunting party had to be a wild card, but she promised to be the lucky charm I needed. Constantly scrutinizing our strategy, we upped our game for that night. The only things visible on us were the whites of our eyes. The night grew cool. Hope faded. Several hours later, with no sign of Hogzilla, Emma remained quiet and patient. Her fresh assurance of victory bolstered our resolve.

Then, in the hush of the early morning hours, we heard the unsettling crunch of heavy hooves on dead leaves and branches. Hogzilla approached. Tantalizing us, he revealed tiny glimpses of his monstrous head through the edge of the thicket, testing, listening, waiting before finally emerging with hesitant steps.

Bows drawn, arrows poised to fly, Micah and I pulled the triggers at the same time. My arrow struck Hogzilla's back and

Micah's penetrated his neck perfectly. Hogzilla took one step and dropped.

After a moment of sheer shock, we all broke into raucous, undignified celebration, dancing and praising and giving thanks to our Father in heaven. Victory! Oh, sweet victory! Our church family was safe again and, as a close second, my reputation was restored.

We decided to have the staff team over for a pool party so that we could grill and serve up Hogzilla as the main course of a triumphant feast. The death of our worthy adversary would not be wasted. While working the grill, someone asked about the key to successfully defeating this respected foe. I responded with, "Less is more." Our Hogzilla hunting approach evolved. We'd embraced minimalism in increments. Finally, we were reduced to a hunting party of only two or three. Scent-control spray covered us from head to foot. No food. No noise. No extra equipment.

Besides God's favor, which led our prey into our hands, recognizing what held us back and getting rid of it and constantly removing things we didn't need resulted in victory. Getting serious on your journey requires you to constantly re-examine and lose the extra baggage holding you back.

The author of Hebrews changed his method as well. As if he began to realize how many endurance runners came before him, he grouped together several of them, summarizing their acts of faith. Five of the six men mentioned by name came from unlikely places to—by the power of God—become warriors, kings, and judges who ruled over Israel. God honors and anoints the faith of those whom He's called to important leadership roles in places like the military and government. One such man named Gideon fit that bill. Unfortunately, he lived during a time of great moral decline. Although the Israelites had hardened their hearts after forty years of peace, God would show mercy and, in His wisdom, choose just the right person to help them.

> And what more shall I say? For time would fail me to tell of Gideon, Barak, Samson, Jephthah, of David and Samuel and the prophets—who through faith conquered kingdoms, enforced justice, obtained promises, stopped the mouths of lions, quenched the power of fire, escaped the edge of the sword, were made strong out of weakness, became mighty in war, put foreign armies to flight (Hebrews 11:32–34).

God gave Gideon this message: "The Lord is with you, you mighty man of valor!" Then God confirmed His calling through several signs, assuring Gideon He would follow through on His promise. By faith, Gideon bravely destroyed the town's altar built for Baal. Full of wrath because their false idol was destroyed, the Midianites gathered for revenge. Satan attacks when his territory is threatened.

Gideon called his countrymen to arms. Surprisingly, God communicated to Gideon there were too many soldiers. Gideon told those who were afraid to go home. Twenty-two thousand left. Ten thousand courageous remained. God said it was still too many and pruned the number to only 300 men. When you place yourself in God's hands, whatever He gives is enough. It may have freaked Gideon out, but he was willing to trust God with less.

All successful endurance runners are obsessed with dropping unnecessary weight. The common-sense solution is to lose body weight. It's puzzling when athletes spend big money on lightweight carbon bikes and components but refuse to diet. Another good practice is wearing aerodynamic Spandex to minimize wind restriction and prevent entanglement. In one year, I dropped thirty-four pounds to finish a race. I lost fifteen pounds of body weight, bought a lighter bike, and exchanged my heavy Camel backpack full of water for a bottle. I also bit the bullet and wore Spandex.

A weight is something you can choose to hold or choose to drop. It can be anything impeding your progress forward. What are the things keeping you from finishing your race? Here are four common weights many struggle to drop.

BODY ABUSE

Many in the Church point fingers at those who harm their bodies with alcohol and drug abuse but ignore those who indulge in several slices of pie and bowls of ice cream. I've been there. I get it. Once upon a time I was overweight, well north of 200 pounds with high cholesterol. Not only was I modeling poor health for my family, I made it so that there was zero chance of me fulfilling God's calling upon my life. By now you know the Lord didn't leave me there. Through the grace and power of God and a lot of hard work, constant submission, and picking myself up after every fall, the Lord redeemed my body and, more importantly, freed me from this sin.

Not dealing with the sin of gluttony is costing hundreds of thousands of Americans their lives every year. It's now the second leading cause of preventable death in the United States. Food is an addiction just like any other. We need to stop pointing fingers and look in the mirror first. Remove the log from your own eye before trying to remove the speck from your brother's.[1]

Apostle Paul says, "Do you not know that your body is a temple of the Holy Spirit within you, whom you have from God? You are not your own, for you were bought with a price. So glorify God in your body" (1 Corinthians 6:19–20). Your body doesn't belong to you, so manage it well. Honor God by taking care of the gift He's given you rather than throwing it away.

HOBBIES

It's okay to enjoy the pleasures God gives, but it's not okay for those pleasures to own you. God made you with certain tastes, talents, and inclinations to enjoy specific gifts from Him. Whether it's recreation, Tex-Mex food, fantasy football, a foot massage, success at work, social media, hunting, music, video games, entertainment, or shopping, follow the convictions the Holy Spirit gives you.[2] He knows your heart better than you do and knows what will trip you up and keep you from fulfilling His will for your life. So, if the Holy Spirit is nudging you toward giving up something or lessening God's presence in your life, listen and obey. Take the prompting seriously.

Just because it isn't a sin for someone else and doesn't look like a sin to you, that doesn't mean it isn't sinful for you. When you walk in stubborn disobedience, these "good" things can quickly lead to the sin of idolatry. When most of us think of idols, we think of statues. Idolatry has to do with worship; it has to do with surrendering the throne room of your heart to something other than God. The apostle Paul describes eating, drinking, and playing as idolatry in 1 Corinthians 10:7: "Do not be idolaters as some of them were; as it is written, 'The people sat down to eat and drink and rose up to play.'" Eating, drinking, and playing are gifts from the Lord, but our sin twists His gifts into idols.

Spending too much time at work can be a way that you find your identity and significance, or you might believe it to be the only way to make a living. There will always be more to do, so you don't have to say yes to everything. I learned a valuable lesson about the importance of delegating responsibilities. Discover your strengths and narrow your focus on what only you can do. Complement your weakness by treasuring those around you.

Search your heart. Ask the Holy Spirit to reveal any idols to you. Overindulgence is a huge red flag. And it can crop up in unexpected, culturally acceptable places. My obsession with a new, healthy lifestyle drove me from one extreme to the other. The pounds were coming off and the means to these results were addicting. There was a season when I was training eighteen hours a week for the IRONMAN TRIATHLON. A couple of years after finishing, someone close to me invited me to get an IRONMAN tattoo. I declined because I had allowed it to become an idol. I'd traded food for exercising. How often do we just trade one idol for another? Only by God's grace can we surrender all to Him and keep the throne room of our hearts open for Him and Him alone.

On the other hand, it's important to remember the Lord doesn't always ask you to lay something down because it's an idol. Instead, there may be times when He asks you to put it aside for a season because He needs you to focus your time and energy elsewhere. Andy Stanley teaches, "Saying yes to something, is saying no to someone else."[3] Resist saying yes to the "weights" and no to those who matter most.

While my kids were young and we were building a permanent home for our growing church family, I made the decision to not participate in any endurance events. During that three-year season, riding my mountain bike only a few times a week was most beneficial to the Lord, my family, and ministry. There will be times when the Lord asks you to lay it down. Surrender. Gifts are not rights. Trust His desire is to give you good things and wait on the Lord.

FINANCES

Debt is like an avalanche blasting through rocks, plowing over trees, and gaining speed until it smothers everything in its path. Debt consumes. Scripture defines it as a form of slavery.[4] When you spend beyond your means, debt becomes a tremendous weight on your shoulders. If you can't pay a credit card off at the end of the month, it's time to cut it up. Resist the temptation to take out loans for something new if you don't already have the savings to purchase it.

You have a responsibility to honor God with money. Remember He is Lord of it, so learn to manage it well. The Bible says more about money than heaven and hell combined. The reason Jesus told so many stories about stewardship is because He knew how much we would struggle with it. Commit to learning biblical financial principles through a good program like Financial

Peace University by financial expert Dave Ramsey. Bring the Lord's tithe back to Him, save at least 10 percent, and then live on the rest. Pray for twenty-four hours before every major purchase and ask the Lord if the purchase is a wise decision. Jesus said apart from Him we could do nothing.[5] When we invite God into every area of our lives, He takes our five loaves and two fish and supernaturally blesses them.[6] Include God in all your financial decisions, walk in obedience, and see what the Lord does.

EMOTIONAL STRONGHOLDS

Emotions are powerful. They are good. They are a gift from the Lord. Talent and ability are nothing without them. The Word says those who lead should lead with zeal.[7] God is emotional. His passions and desires are beautiful and He designed us to be the same way. But like every good gift from the Lord, Satan and our fallen nature have corrupted them. The enemy knows taking away our talents or even our ideas is nothing compared to crushing the heart. He knows emotional weights can and will hold you back from finishing your race. What emotional weights are holding you back? Bitterness? Anger? Fear?

Fear is arguably one of the most powerful and influential strongholds of the heart. You will be tempted to believe worrying is a normal response to a difficult situation. Some may even see worry as a sort of wisdom. It's not. Jesus spent a considerable amount of time commanding you not to worry. To do so is to lack dependence and trust in the Lord. You decide to take responsibility for the situation and because you have it in your hands, you are bearing a burden you cannot bear, a weight you were never meant to carry. Worry changes your beliefs and alters the way you see the world. It also changes the way the world sees you.

When you obsess over the negative, you start to look more like an unbeliever. Jesus preached about it in the Sermon on the Mount. He has your best interest at heart. You can leave it at His feet. Jesus knows the answers to your questions of who you will marry, what you are going to do, and where you are going to live. Paul, from a prison cell, encourages believers to not be anxious about anything and to pray.[8] Fear quenches faith, destroys hope, and suffocates love. Embracing fear means letting go of God. But when you embrace God, His perfect love will cast out your fear. Set your eyes on the only One who can carry your burdens and lay them down at His feet.

What weight is holding you back? It's probably the one thing you will be tempted to obsess over. Jesus expressed it this way: "If anyone would come after me, let him deny himself and take up his cross and follow me" (Matthew 16:24). Drop the dead weight. Surrender it at the feet of Jesus so you can say yes to the best. Give up something good for something great. Choose Jesus as your source of strength, passion, and peace, and in Him you will finish the race.

13

DON'T LET SUCCESS GET TO YOUR HEAD

BARAK

Nearly all men can stand adversity, but if you want to test a man's character, give him power.

Abraham Lincoln

"I DON'T WANT THE RACE T-SHIRT, PODIUM SPOT, OR FINISHER'S medal," said no one ever.

Striving to be your best isn't wrong, but unhealthy ambition for success will keep you from finishing. In my quest to learn from great endurance athletes, I read a book[1] by Lance Armstrong, a Texan who survived cancer to win a record number of Tour de France victories. At a young age, his mother told him, "If you're going to get anywhere, you're going to have to do it yourself, because no one is going to do it for you." Through hard work and intense training, Lance developed a superior VO2 max that was second to none. Also called "maximal oxygen consumption," VO2 max reflects an athlete's endurance capacity during prolonged exercise. But this monumental achievement was not enough. His drive to be the best tempted him to compromise his integrity. As a result, Lance doped, cheated, and then lied about it. Unlike truth, lies don't last forever. Pride and hubris cost him his dignity, his Tour de France yellow jerseys, the right to race again, and his marriage.

Lance isn't alone. History is littered with many who allowed success to get to their heads, resulting in the loss of what they found most dear. Alexander the Great is one such example. The youngest world conqueror rose to eminence in a short amount of time, but Alexander the Great allowed success to twist his view of himself. As a result, he exalted himself above the rest of humanity, declaring himself to be a god. Once a self-disciplined and generous leader, Alexander became cruel, ruthless, and vicious, a corrupted shadow of his former self. During a drunken brawl, in an impetuous act of cruelty, he even murdered a loyal friend who once saved his life. His rapid, downward spiral did not escape God's attention. Alexander's life ended in a sudden, unexpected death at the age of thirty-two. God's judgment arrived. Most historians agree Alexander's death was due to a common disease caused by the bite of a mosquito. Alexander the Great, the man who ruled the known world, was brought low by an insect. The writing was on the wall; God's judgment arrived and Alexander was "weighed in the balances and found wanting."[2]

Pride is the enemy's most effective strategy to keep you from finishing. A bloated ego tempts you to believe you don't need anyone, including God. Don't think success is evidence you've crossed the finish line. The Lord's ways are not our ways, and His ways are higher than our ways.[3] Your idea of success isn't the same as God's. King Saul thought success meant sacrificing animals he was supposed to put to the sword. It cost him his throne and his legacy.[4] Solomon thought himself above his own advice when he preached against adultery in Proverbs only to end up worshipping the pagan gods of his 700 wives and 300 concubines.[5] As a result, God tore Israel out of the hands of Solomon's son and split the kingdom in two, leaving only one tribal kingdom to Solomon's descendants. Perhaps Hebrews 11 doesn't mention Saul or Solomon because they started well but allowed pride to disqualify them from finishing. Instead of a famous king, the author next lists someone you may never have even heard of.

"Barak who through faith conquered kingdoms" (Hebrews 11:32–33).

During the time when Deborah served as Israel's spiritual judge, God used her to give a prophetic word to a soldier named Barak. He listened and courageously obeyed. Perhaps it was this God-given humility that kept Barak from letting success go to his head. Here was a man of honor who understood the authority of God.

Did Saul fall during a difficult time? What about Solomon? Both failed at the height of success. Don't make the mistake of thinking testing only happens in the wilderness. It was in the Promised Land that the Israelites didn't fully obey God and wipe out all the people God told them to put to the sword. As a consequence, people like the Philistines tormented, corrupted, and destroyed thousands afterward. Most who fail do so at the summit. Success is dangerous because it fogs the mind, deceiving you into thinking you need no one, not even God.

Discover from Barak's example how to manage success without allowing it to take you out.

OBEY GOD'S PLAN, NOT YOUR OWN

"Has not the Lord, the God of Israel, commanded you, 'Go, gather your men at Mount Tabor, taking 10,000 from the people of Naphtali and the people of Zebulun'" (Judges 4:6). Deborah gave this prophetic word of God to Barak. Try convincing 10,000 people to fight against a bigger army. Obeying God requires courageous, unrelenting faith.

Runners in life will be tempted to take shortcuts. This happens when you depend upon yourself. My friend and author Mark Batterson writes, "We are so busy climbing the ladder of success that we fail to realize it's leaning on the wrong wall." When you are dependent on your own plan, self-centered pride will invade your soul and tempt you to make unwise decisions.

You must truly believe "apart from God you can do nothing" (John 15:5). Depend upon the power of God to obey His plan for your life. Jesus commands his followers to go and make disciples. This great plan requires great power. It's why the Lord baptizes His followers in the Holy Spirit. Obeying a great purpose will require you to depend on God's ability rather than on your own.

TRUST GOD FOR VICTORY

"And I will draw out Sisera, the general of Jabin's army, to meet you by the river Kishon with his chariots and his troops, and I will give him into your hand" (Judges 4:7). Barak probably ran this promise from the Lord over and over in his mind to bolster his faith. He had to resist being dependent on his 10,000 fellow soldiers. Success means trusting God first and foremost. You will be tempted to trust in what you see. What happens if you don't have enough money? What happens if you don't have enough people? "Some trust in chariots and some in horses, but we trust in the name of the Lord our God" (Psalm 20:7). Trust in God for victory no matter what you see.

After a season of growth, my friend Doctor James Bradford invested a week of ministry into our church family. Like Deborah the prophetess, he gave us this word of warning: "Like many before you, don't let success be your undoing. Don't be dependent upon your systems and processes. Stay hungry for God." It was a difficult message. The Holy Spirit instantly reminded me of the letter given by Jesus to the church of Sardis. "I know your works. You have the reputation of being alive, but you are dead. Wake up, and strengthen what remains and is about to die, for I have not found your works complete in the sight of my God" (Revelation 3:1–2).

Later that evening, I stood in an auditorium full of our staff team and small group leaders to warn about drifting from what was most important and not making prayer our most important priority. We humbled ourselves and asked the Holy Spirit to guide us. In our spirits, we felt the Lord calling us to change the format of our staff team meetings. Instead of beginning with vision and strategy, we would start with worship, prayer, and devotion. Elevating the spiritual practices over the practical reveals how much you rely on God. The pressure and temptation to find comfort and peace in your provisions and systems is enormous, especially as the Lord uses those tools to build success over time.

DEPEND ON OTHERS

"Barak said to her, 'If you will go with me, I will go, but if you will not go with me, I will not go'" (Judges 4:8). When Barak listened to God's plan, he didn't run to his closet for his sword. He valued the importance of Deborah. She was the one who heard from God. He recognized he shouldn't go on this journey by himself.

When *Outreach Magazine* announced Gateway was the fastest growing church in America, I was filled with both gratitude and fear. I was in a tough spot. The enemy wanted to use this to puff me up with pride. I honestly didn't quite know how to respond, so I didn't. As a team, we chose to never speak of it publicly during a weekend worship service. Weeks later, I wrote this to our church family:

> We haven't posted or said anything publicly due to my concern about this going to our head. Quite honestly, it's kind of awkward. It's just a number. But that number and "success" can be the greatest enemy to our mission and the humble spirit required to fulfill it. Let's be quick not to rob, but give God ALL His glory. Let's never forget we started in a living room and spent seven years hauling around beat up, portable cases to set up our church in the dark so we could worship the Lord in a school and movie theatre. As pastor, I unfortunately get mentioned most, but there is no "I" in team. Your staff team of pastors, directors, small group leaders, and volunteers unselfishly serve and love you. They deserve the credit. God is adding to our

> church family because a whole bunch of you are making discipleship your heartbeat like it is thumping fast in Jesus' chest right now. Thank you for not being a "fast growing" church, but a "loving" church where my own three children have a strong relationship with Jesus and you! With many tears, this has become one of the greatest answers to a nine-year-old prayer. Let's never forget our "why." It's all about Jesus and changed lives.

When you do something good, don't believe it was all about you and don't let your mouth get in the way. When someone congratulates you, be quick to answer honestly if you put hard work in. But remember who enabled you to work by giving you talent, time, and opportunity. Defer the praise to the Lord and others. Not only will you be telling the truth, the practice of spreading praise will protect your head and heart. Albert Einstein says, "Success isn't about what you achieve yourself, it's the value you give others." Glorify God above all else. And appreciate, celebrate, honor, and recognize others around you when success is achieved.

NEVER ROB GOD OF HIS GLORY

"And she said, 'I will surely go with you. Nevertheless, the road on which you are going will not lead to your glory, for the Lord will sell Sisera into the hand of a woman'" (Judges 4:9). God inspired Deborah with a prophetic word because many victorious soldiers would celebrate with a party and take all the credit. Charles Spurgeon says, "Christians are not so much in danger when they are persecuted as when they are admired."

Our challenge as believers is fighting the inclination to side with our culture's idea of success. Every worldly definition of success in this world is a lie. Jesus is *the* Truth.[6] Everything not of Jesus is deception. Don't give in to America's version of success. It's not making a lot of money, winning awards, climbing the corporate ladder, possessing power, or gaining a great title. It's not being the valedictorian, going pro as an athlete, or about how many followers or likes you have on social media. So, what is success in the eyes of the Lord?

As a driven, Type A individual, I confess to the dark side of struggling with success during my twenties and thirties. The Clifton Strength Finders test revealed my second strength after "Futuristic" as "Achiever." It helped explain my drive and constant desire for achievement. If I didn't see results, I didn't feel successful. Unfortunately, I fought this sinful slant most days. Everything became a competition. No board game was safe for my family. Losing was unacceptable. Nothing was ever enough. My constant discontent burned inside of me like a relentless wildfire. I had to achieve more. It was a constant tension between acting as a blessing or a curse.

The game changer happened when I finally understood the real definition of success. What does it mean to be *successful*? Jesus defines success in his response to James and John: "But it shall not be so among you. But whoever would be great among you must be your servant, and whoever would be first among you must be a slave of all. For even the Son of Man came not to be served but to serve, and to give His life as a ransom for many" (Mark 10:43–45).

Success is gladly taking second place. It's fighting against the flesh's desire to go to the front of the line and instead serve others. It's making others look better than yourself. It's humility.

Humility is the character of God. It must be your nature as well. It won't come easy at first or maybe ever, but you must humble yourself. Andrew Murray says, "Humility, the place of entire dependence on God, is the first duty and the highest virtue of the creature, and the root of every virtue. And so pride, or the loss of this humility, is the root of every sin and evil."[7]

If you don't humble yourself, God will find creative ways to do it for you. One week after the *Outreach Magazine* article was published about our church, we hosted a church planting conference for one hundred ministers. Our building was new. Recommendations during the building process led us to opt for a septic system instead of a centralized sewer system. Engineers promised a well-functioning, robust system that could handle usage from thousands of people. But right in the middle of this event, the septic tank backed up. Poop was coming out every hole and drain. The whole church reeked. People gagged on their way to find trees outside to relieve themselves. The Lord will use anything to remind you that you are not righteous on your own. True success is making God and others greater than yourself. Always place His Kingdom before your own. "But seek first the kingdom of God and His righteousness, and all these things will be added to you" (Matthew 6:33).

DON'T BECOME COMPLACENT

After God delivered Sisera into Barak's hands, Israel didn't hit the cruise control button. "So on that day God subdued Jabin the king of Canaan before the people of Israel. And the hand of the people of Israel pressed harder and harder against Jabin the king of Canaan, until they destroyed Jabin king of Canaan" (Judges 4:23–24). It's interesting that Scripture reveals the Israelites kept going. They didn't give up after some success.

Arguably the most successful women's basketball team was the Tennessee Lady Volunteers who went 39–0 and won a national championship in 1997. Most sports teams fail to win back-to-back championships because they get complacent. Tennessee Lady Volunteers Coach Pat Summitt said, "It's harder to stay on top than it is to make the climb. Continue to seek new goals."[8] The Lady Volunteers won three championships in a row.

Paul writes to a church in Galatia, "And let us not grow weary of doing good, for in due season we will reap, if we do not give up" (Galatians 6:9). Don't stop living. Keep going. If you achieve success, seek God for your next mountain to climb for His glory. Ask Him for your next fight to win.

14

DON'T LET FAILURE GET TO YOUR HEART

SAMSON

Success is not final. Failure is not fatal.
It is the courage to continue that counts.

ANONYMOUS

DNF ARE THREE DEMORALIZING LETTERS EVERY ENDURANCE runner fears. The acronym stands for "Did Not Finish." Yeah, it had been a couple of years since I completed a race, but I was an IRONMAN. No endurance race intimidated me.

One summer our family joined friends for a two-week primitive camping vacation in the San Isabel National Forest in central Colorado. A few of my mountain-bike buddies and I registered for the Silver Rush 50, a fifty-mile, mountain-bike race winding through the heart of the Sawatch Range, which is home to some of Colorado's tallest mountains. It also included time deadlines to get you off the mountain as soon as possible to miss the brutal, daily, afternoon thunderstorms.

The race began with the boom of a shotgun blast as hundreds of my competitors launched into a steep hike, carrying their bikes straight up a ski hill. From the very beginning, there was no way to keep my heart rate in check. I knew it was going to be a long day. It took everything within me to make the twenty-five-mile halfway mark before the deadline. I was depleted but continued. With only twelve miles left, I took a wrong turn, sending me three miles off course, which meant an additional six miles. By the time I made it back, I was out of time.

Discouraged, I coasted down the mountain to joyous shouts, whistles, and clapping from the crowd while others finished around me. But that wasn't the worst part. Giving my cheering family and friends the bad news would be far harder. When I told them I did not finish, I'll never forget the look in my son's eyes. He not only expected me to finish but also to win. At the end of the day, it was my fault. No excuses. I seriously underestimated how important it was to have a strong aerobic base. I let success get to my head from previous races and thought I could wing it. As a result, I failed.

DNF can describe other failures in life. Affairs and out-of-control addictions to alcohol, drugs, pornography, and other traps of the enemy have cost many their most valued relationships, ministry, jobs, and dignity. The Bible is littered with tragic stories of people who began so bravely only to quit in disgrace. Solomon regressed from wisdom to witchcraft. Saul traded his divinely selected position for death by suicide. Judas Iscariot fell from brother to betrayer. Demas gave up and went from devoted disciple to deserter.[1]

This list stands in stark contrast to those people mentioned in Hebrews 11. Most of them also failed at one time or another, but they got back up. They humbled themselves, repented, and kept the faith. Everyone loves a good comeback story.

Now we'll explore the tragic but amazing comeback story of Samson. Do you remember being inspired by his heroic acts recorded in the Book of Judges? Samson was born with a purpose: deliver his Israelite countrymen from the Philistines. The Lord promised if he never cut his hair, he would be entrusted with incredible strength. Even his name means "Man of the Sun" for crying out loud.

Samson's strength could only be described as supernatural. God empowered him to tear lions to shreds and to defeat an entire squad of soldiers with the jawbone of a donkey. He became a mighty judge of Israel, but all this success went to his head. Eventually, after much persuasion from his manipulative lady, Delilah, he told her the secret of his Herculean power: his Nazarite oath to never cut his hair.

It was his downfall.

Delilah gently put him to sleep on her lap then cut his hair and "began to torment him, and his strength left him."[2] As a result, Samson lost everything—his strength and, far worse, the favor of God. The Philistines captured him, gouged out his eyes, and imprisoned him. Samson could have remained in chains, consumed with regret and bitterness, but instead his failure cultivated humility in him and dependence upon God.

"And what more shall I say? For time would fail me to tell of... Samson... who through faith ... put foreign armies to flight" (Hebrews 11:32–34).

Praise God, Samson's story didn't end there. One day the Philistines gathered in a temple to worship their false god, Dagon. They brought Samson in to mock him and the one true God of the Israelites. The Philistines were packed wall-to-wall on the ground floor, and Judges 16 records there were 3,000 who stood gathered on the roof to watch and heckle Samson. The echoing noise and jeers must have been overwhelming. But Scripture records Samson's hair had begun to grow again.[3] Blind and hobbling, his body impoverished by imprisonment and malnutrition, Samson asked permission to rest his hands against two supporting pillars.[4]

He cried out to the Lord, "O Lord God, please remember me and please strengthen me only this once, O God, that I may be avenged on the Philistines for my two eyes." He then leaned with God's strength against the two pillars and declared, "Let me die with the Philistines." The temple fell and "those whom he killed at his death were more than those whom he had killed during his life."[5] His final act of faith became his most memorable.

If you've failed, know it's not over with you either. Your past mistakes don't doom your future. Stop the pity party, take responsibility, and look ahead. Don't be afraid. God is on your side. Apply these principles so you too can experience a comeback.

FAILURE DOESN'T DEFINE YOU

What separates the good from the great is an unwillingness to give up after failure. Look struggle right in the eye and don't flinch. Walt Disney was fired by a newspaper editor because he lacked imagination. Then his first business went bankrupt. Jim Carrey was so poor he dropped out of high school at age fifteen to get a job as a janitor. When he began to pursue stand-up comedy, he was booed off a stage in Canada. Michael Jordan went home, dejected and wracked by tears, after not being selected as a sophomore for the varsity basketball roster. Oprah Winfrey was fired from a local television station by a producer because she was "unfit for television." J. K. Rowling was depressed from unemployment, the loss of her mom to disease, her divorce, the poverty that resulted from her divorce, and the difficulty of paying bills for the sake of her child. Twelve publishers rejected her first Harry Potter manuscript. When she finally found a publisher, she was told to not quit her day job because authors of children's books didn't make much money. Bill Gates suffered failure in his first business, Traf-O-Data. Pastor and author Mark Batterson's first church plant in Chicago didn't survive. Henry Ford went bankrupt twice. Over 1,000 people told sixty-two-year-old Colonel Sanders his crazy, fried chicken idea would never work. Thomas Edison failed over 10,000 times before he successfully invented the light bulb. When asked by a newspaper reporter if he felt like a failure, Edison replied, "Why would I feel like a failure? And why would I ever give up? I now know over 9,000 ways an electric lightbulb will not work. Success is almost in my grasp."

In almost every area of my life, I have fallen on my face. My cycle of sexual sin as a young man broke the heart of God, but He forgave me and, in time, granted me freedom. I failed as a husband and a father, but grace covered that too. I lost self-control with my weight. I've let others down and made more stupid ministry mistakes than I care to mention. However, every day I choose to deny my past and the shame that comes with it. I look forward to the opportunity of a better future. Don't focus so much on the failure in your past. You will lose sight of your future.

All believers are marked by failure, but all could be marked by perseverance as well. Scripture states, "For the righteous falls seven times and rises again, but the wicked stumble in times of calamity."[6] You might be down, but it's time to get back up and keep moving. You haven't stopped breathing, so God isn't done with you yet. Use failure as a motivator for growth and success. With the Lord and a repentant, humble heart, we always have hope and a future.[7] Don't scorn the discipline of the Lord. He only disciplines those He loves. And when you allow it to train you and shape you, the Word promises it will bring the peaceful fruit of righteousness.[8] Your biggest mistakes can be the catalysts to motivate you to fulfill your God-given purpose.[9]

FAILURE WILL DEVELOP YOU

The bigger the failure, the bigger the lesson. When you fail, it's an opportunity to die to yourself and let a part of your sinful self go six feet under. Don't waste it. Let that death be worth it. Don't let discouragement set in too long. Have a day when you mourn your sin, but dust yourself off and get back up. Jesus said you're blessed if you mourn your sin,[10] not if you pet it and glorify it in a twisted sense of martyrdom. Don't be in love with your sadness. Don't build an altar to your failure. Learn from your mistakes. Take the bad with the good.

What if your failure is so bad you don't think God could ever forgive you? If you feel alone in your temptations, remember you have a High Priest in Jesus who sympathizes with your weaknesses. You have One who was tempted in *every* way, just as you are—yet without sin.[11] In Jesus, we see a new way. He is your greatest Corrector and your greatest Comforter.[12] Don't despair when trials come. Jesus said they must come for testing is the furnace to fashion you into gold, the crucible to craft you into silver, and the pressure to perfect you like a diamond.[13] But when your worst temptation comes, remember 1 Corinthians 10:13: "No temptation has overtaken you that is not common to man. God is faithful, and He will not let you be tempted beyond your ability, but with the temptation He will also provide the way of escape, that you may be able to endure it."

Let your failure become your greatest teacher. Allow that sting to help you avoid the same pitfalls in the future. Facing your weaknesses reveals the weapons and strategies of the enemy and will equip you for warfare. It's not enough to know how God designed you. You must also know how sin twisted you. Look in the mirror. Take a good, long look. It may not be pretty, but humility and brokenness are the best fruits of failure. God will shape your character more during your messes than during your successes. In the hands of the Lord, nothing goes to waste. Face those demons head on and get the help you need to heal, grow, and get better.

REDEEM THE NEGATIVE INTO THE POSITIVE

My dad preaches a sermon called Take the Stick You Got Hit with and Beat the Devil with It. Use what the devil tried to destroy you with and turn it around as a testimony of God's goodness to both encourage and warn others. It's amazing how many people God will bring into your path who are struggling with the same stranglehold Satan used to almost take you out. The two most powerful words you can say to your pain partner are "Me too." If you need support from a friend, you should seek out one who has gone through the same fire and still smells like smoke.

To come so far and not finish what God wants to do in and through you would be your greatest tragedy. When you're in a dark cave and your mind is obsessed with the hundreds of reasons why you should quit, ask yourself this question: "What do I want my story to be?" Did you come to race and quit or to finish? How do you want your children and friends to remember you?

The journey to your highest potential is often straight through the valley of your greatest failure. If you're going to finish, you must believe your failure isn't the end of your story. If you think all hope is gone and God can't use you anymore, you don't really know God's love and character like you thought you did. God loves to redeem the lost, to bind the wounded, and heal the brokenhearted.[14] He loves to take what others meant for evil and use it for good.[15] He desires to make you into a new creation.[16] Don't believe the lie that failure must happen again. God will give you the power to break the cycle.

GUARD YOUR HEART

The enemy will try to tempt you again in the same area of your life where the Lord was glorified through your redemption. You must focus on protecting your heart. "Guard your heart above all else, for it determines the course of your life" (Proverbs 4:23). Place boundaries that will help you remain pure. Find mentors you can trust and empower them to be your accountability partners. "Where there is no guidance, a people falls, but in an abundance of counselors there is safety" (Proverbs 11:14). Don't hang out with the same people who influenced your downfall. Don't go to the same places where you will be tempted. Be wise with what you place in front of your eyes or ears.

The biggest mistake you can make is quitting after a failure. That may be the only time you really fail. Let it become the spark for growth and change to fuel you for better things in your future. The pain of not finishing the Silver Rush 50 was hard for me, but it became a catalyst to do better the next time. I came back the following year to finish strong, and the celebration with my family was so sweet. In Jesus, yours will be too.

How you respond to failure will determine how you finish. Through the redemptive power of God, your best days are in front of you. Don't allow the fear of failing again or the shame keep you from getting back up. There is victory in Jesus. You are a finisher!

15

GRIT

JEPHTHAH

Your finish line is on the other side of your grit.

THE UNDERDOG IS EVERYONE'S FAVORITE. THERE'S SOMETHING exhilarating about watching "the little guy" overcome the odds to claim victory. But what if the underdog gives everything he or she has and doesn't win? Is the underdog still inspiring? I think so. Sometimes, not winning makes the underdog even more inspiring. It's the grit to fight on despite failures and setbacks that etches someone's story in stone.

John Akwari ran the marathon in Mexico during the 1968 Summer Olympics for the pride of Tanzania. Akwari didn't win a medal. In fact, he finished last. He'd never trained at a high altitude and didn't expect the soaring temperatures. The marathon began at 3:00 p.m. during the hottest part of the day. Seventeen of the seventy-four runners never finished the race due to heatstroke and dehydration. Before the race was even halfway over, Akwari's body seized up, wracked by excruciating cramps. Later he took a hit from another runner and fell. While on the ground, several runners trampled him. The medical staff urged him to quit, but Akwari would not.

Four hours after the race began and an hour after the winner crossed the finish line, the closing ceremonies had drawn to a close. Most attendees had already left when the wail of emergency sirens sounded in the distance. Those who remained wondered what was happening. Soon, flashes of bright lights appeared over the horizon. A motorcade slowly approached. The curious spectators watched transfixed as a lone runner came into view, stumbling after the line of vehicles. John Akwari, visibly in severe pain and covered in bloody bandages, staggered across the finish line.

When reporters asked him why he didn't give up, Akwari replied, "My country did not send me over 11,000 kilometers to start the race. They sent me over 11,000 kilometers to finish it." He demonstrated grit and an unstoppable will to finish no matter what, inspiring thousands for decades to come.

Life is a marathon. When you hit resistance, you must have something powerful inside you that causes you to clinch your fists, endure the pain, and inch closer to your finish line. It's a mental toughness that refuses to give up. Grit pays off.

Our next biblical endurance runner came from an obscure, "little guy" beginning, but he finished as a giant of the faith. Few have heard of Jephthah, so why did the author of Hebrews highlight him from a list of over 3,000 Old Testament options?

"For time would fail me to tell of Jephthah" who through faith "conquered kingdoms, enforced justice, obtained promises...made strong out of weakness," and became "mighty in war [and] put foreign armies to flight" (Hebrews 11:32–34).

This unlikely underdog possessed grit. His resolve set him apart. Grit has been defined as an abrasive particle and a firmness of character or unsinkable spirit. It's the persevering passion to fulfill a goal no matter the obstacle in its way. Grit is a driving force. When it's patiently embraced, it can become a pearl. Stephen King writes, "Talent is cheaper than table salt. What separates the talented individual from the successful one is a lot of hard work." Ability is important, but researchers and psychologists agree that higher achieving individuals are driven by a strong determination despite adversity. Discover from Jephthah how to develop more grit in your life to help you finish.

GRIT OVERCOMES THE ODDS

The afternoon I told a close friend I sensed God was calling me to resign my job to start a new church, I overheard his wife ask him if he thought Stephanie and I had what it would take to be lead pastors. Scripture says the wounds of a friend, like discipline, are "faithful;" they are given to support and nourish.[1] But these unforgettable words became a chip on my shoulder. The enemy reminded me of them when I crossed state lines with my family while pulling a U-Haul trailer. The enemy reminded me of them when few pastors in my new community returned my phone call requests to become friends. The enemy reminded me of those words when Gateway began as just a small group of eight friends and family members in the living room of our rental house. However, the voice of the enemy will only be louder than the voice of God when you allow it. The Lord didn't leave me there to be tortured by those words forever. In time, He healed me, removed my shame and that chip on my shoulder, strengthened me, confirmed me, and established me.[2] Whenever I experienced failure or discouragement, the Holy Spirit brought these words to my mind: "God does not despise small beginnings."[3] God also never allows me to forget my small beginnings because to do so would mean to stray from an important place of humility.

Jephthah was the child of a prostitute. According to Hebrew law, this shameful status excluded him and his family from entering a sacred place of worship.[4] Because he was born illegitimately, his half-brothers rejected him as well. As a result, "Jephthah fled from his brothers and lived in the land of Tob, and worthless fellows collected around Jephthah and went out with him."[5]

Who were these "worthless fellows" that are mentioned? They may have been considered worthless by others but not by God. One of the first people I asked to join our new church launch team was the most loyal friend I'd known since high school, Peter Iacona. I tried to "wine and dine" him with a big, juicy burger at the Longhorn Café before I made the big ask. He politely responded, "You don't want me. I've been out of church for a long time. I'm not close to God anymore." I replied with, "You're exactly who God wants." He eventually said yes to being our set-up team director. He used his truck to humbly and faithfully haul our trailer full of equipment for years. Peter married a sweet lady named LeeAnn at our church. They became two of our most fruitful small group leaders.

My favorite baseball player is second baseman Dustin Pedroia of the Boston Red Sox. He makes up for his small stature by a strong work ethic. I saw this with my own eyes on vacation when I met him at a pool. Because Dustin is only five foot nine, only those of us who belong to the Red Sox Nation would recognize him as a celebrity. Even on a holiday, he was up early running and working out. It may or may not be true that I was stalking him. Even enemy number one, the Yankees's Mariano Rivera, said of him, "Nobody plays harder, gives more, wants to win more. He comes at you hard for twenty-seven outs. It's a special thing to see. If I have to win one game, I'd have a hard time taking anybody over Dustin Pedroia as my second baseman."[6]

No status is too low for God's grace. Gideon was a farmer. Barak was a soldier. David was the youngest of his family and disregarded in a field while taking care of sheep. Samuel was a child. Peter was a fisherman. God loves to take underdogs off the bench and call them into the game. Jesus came from the backwoods town of Nazareth,[7] a place from where no prophet would arise from, a place that made some question whether anything good could come from it.[8] He didn't receive respect from anyone in his hometown either.[9] Don't be surprised or take it personally if people doubt you like my friends doubted me. If some doubted Jesus, some will doubt you.

What voice will you listen to when God says it's time to get off the bench? The voice of the enemy says, "You're too young." The Lord says, "Let no one despise you for your youth, but set the believers an example in speech, in conduct, in love, in faith, in purity."[10] The enemy whispers, "Your ethnicity will hold you back." The Lord declares, "For God shows no partiality."[11] The enemy says, "Your gender disqualifies you." The Lord promises, "I will pour out my Spirit on all flesh, and your sons and your daughters shall prophesy, even on my male servants and female servants in those days I will pour out my Spirit, and they shall prophesy."[12] The enemy says, "You're a single parent." The Lord reminds you He is with you always and your children are His children.[13] The enemy says, "You're too ordinary to be used by God." The Lord reminds you He overlooked religious experts to select average fishermen and tax collectors. The enemy says, "You're not smart enough." The Lord says He "chose what is foolish in the world to shame the wise . . . chose what is weak in the world to shame the strong."[14]

GRIT IS DEPENDENCE UPON THE LORD

When Israel was threatened by a nearby country, Jephthah told the elders of Gilead, "If you bring me home again to fight against the Ammonites, and the Lord gives them over to me, I will be your head" (Judges 11:9). Jephthah was either crazy or confident God would be on his side. He knew to them he was an outsider who didn't get much respect. But he made a bold request anyway and knew if he was going to be victorious, it would be because of the Lord's favor and not the favor of man.

Often the Lord transforms your weaknesses into strengths. What the enemy tried to take you out with can be turned into a strength through the power of God. "My grace is sufficient for you, for my power is made perfect in weakness" (2 Corinthians 12:9). The key is to be patient, forgive those who've hurt you, and trust the Lord through His process and timing.

GRIT POSSESSES STRONG FAITH

Imagine Jephthah's experience of recruiting an army and leading them into battle as underdogs. The preparation, journey, and fight were hard work requiring an incredible amount of trust and faith in the Lord. God blessed Jephthah's faith by defeating the Ammonites. And then Jephthah was quick to give glory for the victory to the Lord. Jephthah knew it was God who delivered his countrymen from their oppressors.[15]

Akwari was the twentieth-century hero of Tanzania, but history reveals yet another Tanzanian hero from an earlier time. In the late 1800's, Doctor David Livingstone was an explorer and medical missionary in Africa.[16] One of his callings was to fight for the freedom of slaves. David travelled to Zanzibar, an island off the coast of Tanzania. There, while in Stone Town—an old section of Zanzibar—he made a plea to abolish slavery and the inhumane trafficking of humans that occurred regularly in the market. People from Africa were sold at auction to Arabs who took them from their home and families to the Middle East. David worked hard for the calling God placed on his life, but that hard work became lighter because of his faith in God. He said, "The sweat of one's brow is no longer a curse when one works for God, but actually a blessing."

I've had the privilege of traveling twice to Zanzibar. The purpose of those mission trips was to partner with local pastors to plant new churches in persecuted areas and then equip them with Bibles in their own Swahili language. The effects of Livingstone's hard work over one hundred years before were visible everywhere. A church is currently located on Mkunazini Road in the center of Stone Town. It occupies a large area where the slave market used to be. The constructed church building was a celebration to mark the end of slavery in Zanzibar. An altar now stands in the exact place where the main "whipping post" used to be. It's a powerful witness and testimony. It says, "No matter what you encounter, never give up." Emotions will come and go, but grit is what pushes you through to the end. You will get tired, but grit is what keeps you awake.

GRIT DOESN'T QUIT WHEN IT GETS HARD

Success got to Jephthah's head and he made a bold promise: "whatever comes out from the doors of my house to meet me when I return in peace from the Ammonites shall be the Lord's, and I will offer it up for a burnt offering" (Judges 11:31). It was an unwise oath made in public to all. Tragically, the victorious Jephthah was met on his journey back by his only daughter. He ripped his clothes and cried out in anguish, "Alas, my daughter! You have brought me very low, and you have become the cause of great trouble to me. For I have opened my mouth to the Lord, and I cannot take back my vow" (Judges 11:35). Here's how the story ends: "the daughters of Israel went year by year to lament the daughter of Jephthah the Gileadite four days in the year" (Judges 11:40).

The Lord isn't a puppetmaster. He allows us to act. And, unless He shows tremendous, undeserved mercy, our own foolishness comes back to torment us. Jephthah could've chosen his daughter over the Lord. Instead, he recognized it was his own foolish pride to blame. He knew it wasn't the Lord's fault his daughter met him at the door, the fault was his own. And he knew the Lord wept along with him in his tremendous grief. As Abraham would've done to Isaac had God not provided a ram, Jephthah remained faithful and obeyed despite the anguish it brought, trusting God's character and believing he would meet his daughter again in paradise. Jephthah persevered in faith no matter the cost. His great love for the Lord allowed him to unknowingly and prophetically live out what our heavenly Father would do with His only Son. The Father promised Adam and Eve He would send a Savior to redeem them. And when the time came for Him to keep His Word and honor His vow, the Lord sacrificed His own Son because of His love for us.

It was Jephthah's faith and grit to endure that carved out a place for him in Hebrews 11. Run your race with grit, refuse to abandon the Lord no matter what, and one day, on the other side, the Lord will tell you, "well done, good and faithful servant."[17] He will also redeem every tear, restore every loss, heal every wound, and glorify you for your perseverance and grit.

16

CONSTANT FORGIVENESS

DAVID

He that cannot forgive others breaks the bridge over which he must pass himself.

GEORGE HERBERT

"I'M SORRY, DAD, BUT I RESIGN."

It is my biggest regret. Stephanie and I ended our two-year journey serving as my dad's youth pastor in Colorado because of an offense. The words and actions of an influential church leader named Tim[1] wounded us so deeply that we questioned if full-time ministry was worth it. Experiencing ugly pain when church folks didn't resolve conflict biblically devastated us. I'll never forget backing our U-Haul truck out of the driveway before dawn and watching my dad in the rearview mirror weep as we drove away. As his form disappeared, lost beneath the pale yellow of the streetlights and then swallowed by darkness, something broke apart inside me and tear-soaked bitterness set in. I was critically wounded and didn't know if the vision God gave me would survive.

Feeling as if I needed to retreat and start over, I enrolled in seminary to pursue a master's degree. Books and classrooms were safe. They wouldn't hurt me. I worked at a golf course a few miles from our apartment. I kept myself busy. It took a couple of years for the wounds to heal enough before I could even consider giving ministry another chance. But in my immaturity, I promised myself I would serve with one rigid stipulation: never get close to a Christian leader again.

I stopped trusting. I showed up with ability and experience, but my heart had suffered too many losses and there was only so much I could give. We opened our hearts to the students and through them we grew, but my choice to never trust adults quickly became a lid on our ministry. My pastor wisely confronted me with an ultimatum: "Forgive and trust or go." I realized I wouldn't change until I recognized the cost. I could no longer drink poison and expect Tim to die instead of me. I needed an internal, supernatural miracle. I humbled myself and asked God to help me forgive Tim.

Ten years later, Stephanie and I brought a team of leaders to a ministry conference in Dallas, Texas, attended by several thousand people. After a general session, I stood waiting in the lobby for my friends to come out. A familiar face caught my eye. I turned to see Tim. My ever-loving wife quickly greeted him with a hug while I wanted nothing less than to blindside him with a punch to the throat.

Wait a minute. Where did those feelings come from? I thought I forgave him. The instinct to exact revenge of some kind only increased, so I turned and walked away before I did or said something stupid.

The next day I chose a breakout session only fifteen people signed up for. I entered the room looking for an empty seat only to find enemy number one—Tim—sitting at the front. Fuming, I turned right back around and left. What was happening?! A couple of hours later, amongst a swarming throng of hundreds of people crammed into the parking lot seeking lunch, Stephanie and I waited in a long line offered by one of a dozen or more food trucks. The person in front of us left the line, leaving me face-to-face with Tim.

It may as well have been high noon with a tumbleweed rolling between us and buzzards circling overhead.

For a moment, the pendulum hung in mid-air. Which way would it go? After a few seconds the tension gave way to a softening of hearts that could have only come from the Holy Spirit. It felt more like a "Fine, God, fine!" than a "Yes, Lord, whatever You want," but I couldn't ignore these miraculous, divine interventions.

In one of those strange moments when no one speaks but there's perfect communication, we nodded at each other and walked behind the church building. Instead of fighting, we confessed our sins. It gave way to a long embrace followed by swollen eyes and tear-streaked faces. Who cared if we looked like a couple of junior high girls? We were free. We finally forgave each other after twenty years and God knew we both needed it.

The next endurance runner mentioned in Hebrews 11 is David, a man who understood what it meant to constantly forgive someone who relentlessly sought his harm. He, like the other endurance runners, was not perfect by any means, but he finished strong. When you think of David, you might first remember him being the underdog, the shepherd boy and surprise choice to be anointed Israel's king. By God's power, David—who was rooted in faith and a passionate love for his Lord—was mighty in battle over Goliath and other armies. He was also mighty in worship. He was mighty because he believed his God was mighty. But David is remembered for another quality.

David had the worst father-in-law of all time—a man named Saul, a jealous and insane boss who tried for decades to hunt him down and kill him. During one of these crusades to take David out, Saul led 3,000 men to seek David's death at a place called the Rocks of the Wild Goats. It was there that nature called and Saul entered a cave to relieve himself. Of all caves, it was the one where David and his men hid. David's men encouraged him to kill Saul, but David submitted to the conviction of the Holy Spirit to not harm the Lord's anointed. Instead, he cut off a corner of Saul's robe as proof of that moment of obedience. When Saul was speechless, dumbfounded at the mercy shown to him, David replied with this ancient proverb, "Out of the wicked comes wicked."[2] Because Saul misunderstood David and the Lord, he expected wickedness from his adversary but found mercy instead. Discover from David how to forgive when others don't deserve it.

BREAK THE BITTERNESS CYCLE

Bitterness is being hurt and unwilling to forgive. It's not by accident the author of Hebrews 11 writes fourteen verses later to a runner finishing his race. "See to it that no one fails to obtain the grace of God; that no 'root of bitterness' springs up and causes trouble, and by it many become defiled" (Hebrews 12:15).

Oak wilt is a problem in the Texas Hill Country. It's a disease that affects oak trees, killing them in droves. Oak wilt begins below the surface in the roots. Outward signs consist of leaf discoloration, wilt, and finally death. The worst part of this disease is its ability to spread to healthy trees by connections between the roots of the oak grove.

Like oak wilt, a seed of hurt grows and festers into something dangerous. It doesn't stop and it spreads to your whole life, killing everything. Take an unforgiving spirit seriously; it's one of the most successful strategies the enemy will use to take you out. The moment you get hurt and choose to hold on to your offense, you start this bitterness cycle.

NEGATIVITY

When you replay the offense over and over in your mind, your attitude becomes negative. You carry the grudge around and nurse it while the other person has long forgotten it. You develop a critical spirit. You stop giving the benefit of the doubt because you only see everything through a lens of hurt. You become irritable and moody. You are so fixated with the hurt that your life is marked by complaining, fault-finding, and gossiping.

REBELLION

Your heart is now hardened. Because you are not walking in submission to God by refusing to forgive as He commands, negativity turns into rebellion. You are no longer teachable and resist those in authority. You begin to do things you know are wrong, but your anger makes it so you don't care. You make excuses for your behavior and rationalize it. You blur the lines and come up with a set of standards no longer aligned with the Bible. Just as oak wilt spreads to other healthy trees, your bitterness spreads and creates bitterness in others because wounded people hurt people. You begin to hang out with people who are hurt, and together you tear others down.

ISOLATION

The cycle continues when you stop trusting others as I did. But the walls you build for self-preservation don't protect. They imprison you, preventing you from receiving the healing you need through the fellowship of other healthy believers. You become silent, but your silence is deafening. Bitterness has wrecked all desire for community. It leads to relational tension with everyone around you. You are afraid to make new friends. When you finally do, it's only a couple who are like you or whom you can control.

DECEPTION

Because you have abandoned God's moral compass and spurned Truth Himself, you slip into deception. You are now in dire need of God's intervention. Deception is a carefully crafted web that not only traps you as a spider traps its prey, it also lulls you into a bewitched slumber, whispering, "All is well. You aren't trapped. You're freer than you ever were before." You stop showing compassion and gratitude. Now you have found a way to not only justify your bitterness but also your hatred. Scripture says if you hate someone, you have committed murder in your heart.[3] You have no right to withhold mercy. Not only does your hatred make you a murderer, your sin also murdered the Son of God. Declaring yourself to be the only one who can tell right from wrong, you place yourself at God's throne of judgment. When you hold back mercy, you show yourself as unfit to receive mercy from God. Deception has twisted you into a vengeful, deluded, self-made god who refuses to surrender control.

DEATH

The bitterness poisoning your spirit passes on to your body and emotions. It leads to anxiety and depression. What is happening deep inside begins to show on the outside. It's revealed by an angry, heavy countenance and hardened facial features. Bitterness spreads and infects every part of you and your life like cancer. "Surely resentment destroys the fool, and jealousy kills the simple" (Job 5:2, NLT). A wounded spirit affects everyone around you. You are responsible for the health of your heart. Once you humble yourself before the Lord and break out of the bitterness cycle, you can take your next step in God's process of reconciliation.

FORGIVE BECAUSE JESUS FORGAVE YOU

Forgiveness of others is not conditional or based on an apology. Even while Jesus hung on a cross, He chose forgiveness. He cried out, "Father forgive them for they know not what they do." It is your responsibility. Your emotions and the degree of offense are not factors either. It's only based on what Jesus did on the cross for you. "Let all bitterness and wrath and anger and clamor and slander be put away from you, along with all malice. Be kind to one another, tenderhearted, forgiving one another, as God in Christ forgave you."[4] Remember how much your sin broke the heart of God? Did God forgive you even when you didn't deserve it? He forgave me of a lot. No one understands more than Jesus what it feels like to be hurt and betrayed, yet he never became bitter. Look to Him.

Conflict is inevitable. Forgiveness is a choice. If you withhold it, Jesus warns you won't be forgiven by the Father.[5] If you are His child, there is no way around it. It's not up for negotiation. But if you extend mercy, you will be blessed and receive it.[6] Besides, you may never look more like Christ than when you forgive. E. Stanley Jones says, "The most blessed fact of the Christian gospel is the offer of divine forgiveness." When you remember how much God forgave you, it will become easier to forgive others.

FORGIVE QUICKLY AND CONSTANTLY

A mark of your spiritual maturity is the short time between hurt and forgiveness. Quick and constant forgiveness requires faith and obedience. Many say with their mouth they forgive but hold resentment in their hearts. Some wait. Others wonder if there is a limit to forgiveness. Even the apostle Peter asked Jesus how many times one should forgive. But Jesus doesn't just demand obedience. He helps us in our weaknesses and this area is no different. Jesus offers us a method for resolving conflict in Matthew 18:15–17. I pray you read it. Meditate on it. Memorize it.

> If your brother sins against you, go and tell him his fault, between you and him alone. If he listens to you, you have gained your brother. But if he does not listen, take one or two others along with you, that every charge may be established by the evidence of two or three witnesses. If he refuses to listen to them, tell it to the church. And if he refuses to listen even to the church, let him be to you as a Gentile and a tax collector (Matthew 18:15–17).

It's not complicated, but it is difficult. Go off alone and before you do anything else, ask the Holy Spirit to reveal how you first hurt God and others. Make a list. Ask God's forgiveness and then ask forgiveness from those you offended, and do it in person if possible. If they've passed away or they're dangerous or there's no way for you to contact them, let alone meet them, write a letter. Humble yourself and say, "I'm sorry. I was wrong. What can I do to make this right so that our relationship is reconciled?" Then burn the list or throw it in the trash. This is a form of confession. Once the part of you killed by an unforgiving spirit is revealed by your confession, let it go.

As a follower of Jesus, develop thick skin and a tender heart. Love is not irritable or easily offended.[7] But if you are honestly, deeply hurt, or if you choose to be offended, go directly and privately in a spirit of humility to win over your sibling in Christ. Reveal your hurt in love. Do as Paul recommends in Galatians 6:1: "Brothers, if anyone is caught in any transgression, you who are spiritual should restore him in a spirit of gentleness." No matter the response, choose to forgive. You must let it go. If that doesn't work, bring a mutual friend to help. Do whatever it takes. Just as wounded people hurt people, forgiven people forgive others. Love keeps no record of wrongs and gives the benefit of the doubt.[8]

FORGIVE YOUR ENEMY

Jesus says to pray for, bless, and love your enemies.[9] He's not providing lip service alone. While hanging on the cross, Jesus said, "Father, forgive them."[10] If Jesus can forgive His enemies, the very people who tortured and murdered Him, He can empower you with the grace to forgive too. It will be a powerful testimony to everyone around you. Forgiveness and love are the crucial marks of every follower of Jesus. Scripture says people will know we're His by our love for each other.[11]

FORGIVE THE FRIEND WHO STUCK A KNIFE IN YOUR BACK

Stephanie and I had a close friend for many years. We vacationed together out of state. We hired this person to be on our church staff with us. We wept together, prayed together, and served the Lord together. But something went wrong. Without our realizing it, something changed in this friend. Later we would find out this person gossiped about us behind our backs, causing division and hurt within our church. The repercussions were devastating. With great pain and sorrow, Stephanie and I sought reconciliation by painfully going through all three steps Jesus commanded of us in Matthew 18. I watched my wife's spirit begin to wither and die over the course of nine months. Her joyful smile and positive attitude disappeared. Seeing her attacked fanned my own pain into fury. My mindset was "You can mess with me, but stay away from my wife and children."

But this person who no longer called us friends refused the restoration process and moved on. I made a list of who betrayed us, who jumped on the attack, who stood by, who abandoned us, and who loyally protected us. I looked at that list every week. It was toxic. It was Tim all over again, but far worse.

A couple of months later, leaders in our church family brought us to the church stage during a leadership Christmas party to honor us. We were presented with a bag filled with sixty cards written from staff and leaders. I carried the bag to my office and violently threw it into a corner. I said I forgave, but I was still wracked with anger. For three long months, I refused to open a single card. I was hurt by someone I trusted in our church family, so I was mad at our whole church. I felt the root of bitterness begin to burrow into my heart, but I didn't want to stop it. I started putting up walls and keeping staff members at arm's length.

Let me tell you, God won't bless an unforgiving spirit. Forgiveness is not easy, but it is doable and worth it. By faith, one day God made a crack in my walls. I looked at that bag of cards, still lying in the corner of my office, and, led by a tiny seed of hope planted by the Holy Spirit, I opened every card and read the words of affirmation and genuine love from my church family. Every hardened part of my heart gave way. I forgave and God restored.

Grief is proportional to intimacy. The closer you are to a person, the more the betrayal will hurt whether it is intentional or not. A friend may have wrecked you with careless words. A family member may have abused you at a young age. Your spouse may have betrayed your trust or committed adultery multiple times. Maybe a trusted friend deceived you. Forgiveness may seem impossible, and, in fact, it is impossible apart from God. I may not know the kind of pain you've endured, but I do understand betrayal. The Lord knew Tim's betrayal and God's healing and forgiveness between us would prepare me for my greatest hurt.

Jesus did no wrong but was betrayed by Judas.[12] Many of his own disciples abandoned him when He needed them most. God understands. Truly. He knows how difficult it is. He will honor your choice to forgive. He will restore you with comfort. Forgiveness is followed by a supernatural peace deep down, all the way to your inner self. That peace will bring peace with others and peace with God. Bitterness isn't the only thing that spreads. Forgiveness and the resulting peace spreads too. Let God settle the score, receive His freedom, and rest in Him.

17

REST TO BE YOUR BEST

SAMUEL

When fatigue walks in, faith walks out.

Dr. Dave Martin

While standing at the Marangu Gate, I, my friend Johnny Hauck, and a few others were ready to tackle a six-day hike up Mount Kilimanjaro, a dormant volcano. It's Africa's highest mountain with a snow-covered summit soaring up to 19,341 feet or over three-and-a-half miles into the sky. Our guide, Jamaica, asked what we expected to find in a successful journey. Nearly all of us responded with two words: "To summit." He then told us stories of hikers so possessed with summit fever that they ignored the symptoms of acute mountain sickness. With a somber expression and quiet words, Jamaica said, "People die on Kili. Success is not summiting. Success is getting back home to your family."

Burnout is ignoring symptoms. It can happen to anyone, especially in ministry. Believing your work overload is good because you're serving God is a lie. Don't believe it. God doesn't want you burned out. He cares about you just as much as the people you are serving. I am saddened by many friends who started well in ministry but quit before their season was over. Even with healthy hours, it's exhausting and hard work. The Barna Group surveyed over 14,000 pastors in a report called *The State of Pastors*. The statistics are alarming. Forty percent of our spiritual leaders are at risk of wearing thin or burning out. Only 34 percent are satisfied with their friendships. Many are lonely and under tremendous pressure, making them vulnerable to attack from the enemy.

Burnout happens outside of ministry too. It seems like many are working hard for too long without faith and rest. It's an epidemic in American society. Another day, another dollar. Time is money. We've even reduced recess in our public schools.

Burnout can also overtake you when you try to be like someone God never intended you to be. You are designed a specific way. Some handle stress and pressure well because they were made that way. Don't look at their example and assume you should be the same way.

Do you feel the signs of burnout? Take a moment and ask yourself the following: Are you tired all the time? Do you not bounce back from sickness like you used to? Are you easily irritated? Do you sleep poorly or have panic attacks? Have you lost your passion or desire for physical activity? Do you feel disconnected, stressed out, or anxious? If you ignore the red flags, burnout is inevitable and it will destroy your emotional, spiritual, and physical health. Your family and work will suffer too.

Samuel, our next endurance runner, lived a life chock-full of achievements, honor, duty, and great acts of faith. But the Bible never mentions even a moment of burnout in his life. His life from beginning to end should have been a recipe for burnout, but it wasn't. Samuel was the product of a desperate mother's prayer. He was literally raised in the Temple of God. When he was eleven years old, the audible voice of God woke him for a word of prophecy.[1] Samuel became the first major prophet. He was granted the honor of anointing David as king and stayed with him as a mentor for many years. If Samuel never burned out, there is hope for you. It is God's will for you to be healthy and passionate, no matter how your life may look. Discover these disciplines to prevent burnout so that you can finish strong like Samuel.

RUN AT THE RIGHT PACE

After five days of hiking up Mount Kilimanjaro, Johnny and I finally reached summit camp and heard the most vital advice we'd receive. Jamaica told us to never forget the phrase "*pole, pole*," which is Swahili for "slowly, slowly." He knew we'd need to hear those words and repeat them in our minds over and over again for the last leg of our journey up the mountain. After a few hours of rest, we began our final, six-hour hike to the summit. Whenever our excitement spurred us to increase the pace, he gently reminded us to take deep breaths and slow down. We couldn't reach the summit on empty; we would need energy for the long hike back down the mountain.

Every long-distance athlete understands the importance of *pole, pole*, of running at a moderate pace. Whenever I competed in anything lasting over ten hours, I constantly checked my pulse monitor so that I never went beyond 75 percent of my maximum heart rate. No matter how good I felt, I had to stay disciplined. Giving in to the temptation to increase my pace by even six beats per minute could mean walking at the end or even a DNF.

Your life of faith is not a sprint, it is a marathon. Marathons require a slower pace. If you go too fast, you'll burn out. In life, finding the right pace and rhythm is critical to finishing strong. You must learn when to drive hard and when to back off. Don't allow others to influence your pace either. Don't give in to comparing yourself or trying to keep up at someone else's pace. You know yourself best so don't increase your pace when outside voices tell you to run faster. Learn the discipline and become good at saying, "No." Operate within your strengths and do the things only you can do.

Moses worked from morning until evening resolving disputes between the Israelites, but he was exhausting himself. His father-in-law saw the effect it was having on Moses and confronted him in a spirit of love. He explained that if Moses kept going at this pace, he would burn out. He instructed his son-in-law to recruit faithful leaders and delegate responsibilities so that everyone could be cared for.[2]

I worked more hours when our church attendance was at 200 than I do now. I couldn't do everything, but if I was going to last, I needed to do the right things. My highest priority was to equip the right[3] leaders and delegate responsibilities so that I could lead in areas of passion, strengths, and gifts to maximize Kingdom impact. Today at Gateway I make disciples, cast vision for the direction of our church family, teach 60 percent of the time, and train leaders. I work smarter, not harder or longer. We are a team-driven church. Our church family has a healthy expectation for our staff. We can't directly care and disciple everyone, but we can create a system where everyone can be loved. A healthy small group culture honors God and takes good care of a growing church family. An unhealthy expectation for a pastor to do all the work of the ministry is a big reason why churches don't grow and leaders burn out.

You must place healthy boundaries and processes in place to protect your schedule. If you don't, others will. Think and plan for sustainability and healthy long-term goals for you and your family. If you ignore priorities and boundaries between your family and ministry, your calendar will be full while your mind, body, and spirit will be empty.

REST

Rest is essential to longevity. The days leading up to a big race event are known as "taper week." By not training as hard, you give your body and mind a chance to prepare for a long day. During a long-distance race, aid stations are for resting and refueling. And during a multiple-day, mountain-bike stage race in the Colorado mountains known as the Breck Epic, resting and recovering become paramount. After long endurance events like this one, athletes will recover when the number of rest days equals the number of hours required to finish the race. If you don't get your rest, you can't be at your best. High performance leaders have a common trait. They eat balanced meals, sleep longer at night, and take regular power naps.

Disobeying God's command to "remember the Sabbath for it is holy"[4] is probably the number one reason why many burn out. God didn't just command it. He modeled it when He rested on the seventh day after six days of work.[5] Honoring His command to take a day of rest is your sacred responsibility. If you were to visit Israel today, you'd discover the entire country shuts down from sunset on Friday to sunset on Saturday. No stores are open. Airplanes stop flying. They obey the Lord. They rest.

Unfortunately, our American culture prides itself on busyness. If you aren't busy, you're considered lazy. Nearly half of the pastors surveyed in a Lifeway Research study admitted they don't take a regular Sabbath.[6] It's an obedience issue. You wouldn't rob God of his sacred tithe, so don't rob Him of this sacred time of rest. A tithe means believing God can do more with your 90 percent than you could do with 100 percent. What if you shared that same belief concerning time? If you are exhausted, remember what Jesus said in Matthew 11:28: "Come to me, all who labor and are heavy laden, and I will give you rest." Rest isn't optional because God knows if you disobey you'll become weary and tired. You won't feel His presence or have the passion needed to fulfill His purpose for your life. You are worth too much to the Lord and His Kingdom. I'm not a Sabbatarian, but I do apply the wisdom of rest.

Before you can help others, you must help yourself. Imagine you are flying on an airplane with your family. If there was a problem that required everyone to reach for an oxygen mask, your first instinct might be to help others. However, the best way to help others is to place your own oxygen mask on first. Scripture makes an interesting connection: "Rest in the Lord and wait patiently for Him" (Psalm 37:7). You have two options.

You can try and do everything yourself in your own strength, leaving you worn out. Or you can rest and be patient for God. When you do, He will give you supernatural strength, wisdom, and power. Resting is a non-negotiable for finishing your race. Consider implementing a system of rest into your schedule.

DIVERT DAILY

Jesus withdrew often to "desolate" places to spend time with His Father in solitude.[7] If Jesus, the Son of Man who was fully God, needed rest, we do too. Make time to connect with the Lord. Consistently caring for your soul is critical to long term health. Don't just block a few minutes in the morning. Be aware of His presence during the day for worship, prayer, and gratitude. Fellowship with God. Walk with Him.

WITHDRAW WEEKLY

My favorite day of the week is Friday because it begins with a mountain-bike ride and ends with a date with my wife. We usually hop on my motorcycle and take a ride to the river where we set up our double nest hammock to cuddle or read a book. It's important to recharge your batteries with a day off that is not filled with work or the "honey-do list." You are uniquely wired. Do what you enjoy that brings joy to your soul. Include a large block of solitude as well. Disable your email. Turn off your phone. Enjoy God's gift of rest with a day off.

QUIT QUARTERLY

Once every few months, consider taking an overnight trip away. A longer block of time for rest, reflection, and recreation is valuable for staying energized. Make it a rule to use all your vacation days no matter what. But what if you don't have a lot of money? Discover the adventure of the outdoors where you can camp in a tent.

When God quickly added many to our church family, we offered six, weekend worship services to accommodate the growth until phase two of our building could be finished. It was a tough season for our leadership team. When we couldn't quite pay market value for staff salaries, we gave the gift of time. In addition to vacation days and the expectation of being home five nights a week, everyone was given six weekends off per year. We worked hard. Played hard. Rested well. The added benefit led to empowering and training more leaders and volunteers to do the work of the ministry.

STAND STILL ON A SABBATICAL

The word "sabbatical" comes from the Hebrew word *shabbat*, which literally means "ceasing." *Shabbat* is mentioned several times in the Bible. The Lord commands the Israelites in one instance to stop working the fields during the seventh year so that the land and the workers could rest.[8] This longer break from work usually lasted from one month to an entire year.

Before Gateway started, my family paid a heavy price for my decade's worth of overworking. I refused to make the same mistake twice. From the very beginning of Gateway, our advisory council prayed about a plan to help our pastors rest so that they could serve with healthy longevity. Their counsel resulted in a plan similar to God's command concerning the seventh year. After every five years of service, every pastor is given a one month sabbatical in addition to vacation time. God takes sabbaticals seriously, so we should too.

After serving our Gateway family for ten years, I learned three lessons during my sabbatical. First, God is in control. Second, you are less important than you think you are. Third, others are more important than you think they are. When you return, your church gets a new pastor and you get a new church. If you want to last for the long haul, put a plan in place. Don't assume you know what you need more than God does.

If you're not in full-time vocational ministry, ask the Holy Spirit to guide you in how to rest in your unique situation. You may not be in control of your schedule and feel like you are burning the candle at both ends. Have an honest conversation with your supervisor about a healthy schedule. Although there are seasons when extra time is required, they should be seasons and not the norm. If you are a supervisor, remember not everyone has the capacity to run at your pace. Sympathetically listen to your direct reports and make sure your employees have blocks of time devoted to rest so that they won't burn out.

Sabbaticals won't happen by accident or on the fly. You must make them a well-thought-out, pre-planned block of space on your calendar. When you see the number of "wasted" days, don't feel guilty. That's the enemy and our culture talking. Silence the voices that are not from God. If you find it challenging to rest for yourself, obey God's command for the sake of others. When you take care of yourself by putting on the “oxygen mask” first, you’ll be able to help others later. The Lord needs you at your best. Your family needs you at your best. You need you at your best. So, rest now before you burn out later.

18

PERSEVERING WITH PRAYER

DANIEL

Prayer does not fit us for the greater works;
prayer is the greater work.
Oswald Chambers

"I NEED YOU. IF YOU HAVE FAITH TO BELIEVE IN GOD FOR A miracle, please meet me tomorrow here at this movie theater parking lot at 7:00 a.m. for a prayer walk."

Forty-eight hours before making this request of our church family that Sunday morning, I sat in the lower level of Ebenezers Coffeehouse listening to pastor Mark Batterson share his story of walking a prayer circle around Washington D.C. God answered his prayers with supernatural provisions. I explained to him our frustration of seeing door after door close for a permanent church home back in San Antonio, Texas.

After worshipping God in homes, then in a school, and then in a movie theater, we'd reached maximum capacity and had nowhere to go. It was a great problem to have, but a problem nonetheless. Mark laid hands on me and prayed for us to stand together upon his experiences and shoulders of faith.

With my mind on the powerful time of prayer I'd spent with my friend a few days before, I wasn't sure what to expect the morning after the big ask. I arrived at the parking lot early on a cool, cloudy Monday morning in October filled with nervous anticipation. Who knew what God would do? Over the next thirty minutes I watched in amazement as seventy-five friends of mine showed up. Looking around at the prayer warrior army the Lord had provided humbled me beyond words. As we prayed hand in hand before making the short trip on foot to the land where we hoped to build a church, it took a great deal of effort to keep my eyes dry.

Strung along in a casual line, we set off down the access road of Loop 1604, following the sidewalk until it ended. Then we walked along a weed-choked deer trail and the lip of a concrete embankment. After about ten minutes, we stood at the edge of our Promised Land: twelve acres of raw Texas beauty appraised at $2.3 million. There was no way we could buy the land and pay for construction. We needed a miracle.

With a unified somberness that came from knowing the financial giant before us, we walked a circle around that land. The land was wild. There were no visible trails, just mesquite, mountain laurel, cedar, and oak groves broken up by occasional meadows and punctuated by prickly sotol and clusters of cacti. In the thick of the tall, willowy grama grass and wild barley, it was hard to tell which direction we were going. We were blazing a new trail in more ways than one. We also came across several illegal dump sites littered with broken glass, abandoned tires, stained mattresses, charred lawn chairs, and abandoned firepits.

But the true battle wasn't over the untamed landscape. Its state was merely a physical example of the spiritual battle before us. We walked and prayed desperate prayers, some aloud, some only heard by the Lord.

Once we made it back to the parking lot I asked if anyone could come to walk and pray again tomorrow. The next morning, we embarked on another prayer walk. Then another. And another. On the fourteenth day of praying circles, I led our church family on a different path from the one we'd made. After so many days, I was trying my best to be creative. We found ourselves in the middle of thick brush. I noticed a shed deer antler on the ground. When I picked it up, the Holy Spirit reminded me of the ram caught in the thicket when God provided a miracle of provision for Abraham.

In the Spirit I proclaimed, "God, You are our Provider!" Immediately afterward, an eleven-year-old girl screamed at the sight of a snake only six inches from my face. This demon from hell had coiled itself around a low-hanging cedar branch. Because we had so many children with us, the instinct to protect launched me into immediate action. Without pause, I grabbed the snake around its neck, rebuked it, and threw it as far as I could. It was the Lord in me because in hindsight that was crazy! But again, this interaction was a physical example of a spiritual battle. Everyone witnessed and sensed the weight of the moment and began to pray against anything preventing God's blessing.

The very next day, God provided the ram.

The Green family, the owners of Hobby Lobby, heard about our story and made a generous offer on the land. The owner accepted it, and the Green family donated all the land to us with no strings attached. It was a modern-day miracle so that God could be glorified.

How many miracles are missed because we give up the call to pray too early? Lack of prayer is dangerous. It reveals weak or lazy faith and an underwhelming, diminished view of the power of God. You may feel too busy to pray or not quite sure what you should say or even how to pray. Discover from the next endurance runner the method and power available through prayer when it becomes a priority. The author doesn't mention him by name but gives a clue, describing how by faith he "stopped the mouths of lions."[1] Only one person fits this description.

When Daniel heard the news of how the king signed a law forcing everyone to worship a false god, he faced a serious decision. Because Daniel feared God more than man, he made the right decision. "He got down on his knees three times a day and prayed and gave thanks before his God, as he had done previously."[2] As a penalty for his refusal to back down, the king commanded that Daniel be cast into the den of lions.[3] But this brave prophet's story didn't end there. God not only delivered Daniel because of His mercy but also because of Daniel's unwavering conviction and faith-fueled prayers.

Faith and prayer are links in a chain. Without prayer, there is no "stopping the mouths of lions." Much is at stake. "Be watchful. Your adversary the devil prowls around like a roaring lion, seeking someone to devour."[4] The enemy's mouth is open with his teeth exposed and his claws extended, trying to tear you down with gossip or lies and accusations. Discover how prayer is essential for both a relationship with God and for ministry.

PERSONAL PRAYER

Prayer is simply a conversation with God. It's pouring your heart out and listening to what is on His. When you consistently pray, your faith and intimacy with Christ grows. Your closest friends are those with whom you intentionally spend the most time.

The Holy Spirit inspired the author of Hebrews to reveal the method and persevering prayers of another endurance runner. "In the days of His flesh, Jesus offered up prayers and supplications, with loud cries and tears, to Him who was able to save Him from death, and He was heard because of His reverence" (Hebrews 5:7). Followers of Jesus saw the power of God come from His prayers. It was difficult for them to understand at times, but they witnessed its mighty effectiveness. The Gospels don't reveal them asking Jesus how to preach, heal, perform miracles, or teach, but we know they did ask Jesus how to pray.[5] They learned from Jesus that the anointing for ministry flowed from intimacy with the Father.

Jesus doesn't leave you in the dark. Most people already know the Lord's Prayer. But if you look at His words before the Our Father, you'll find even more in-depth instruction. "And when you pray, do not heap up empty phrases as the Gentiles do, for they think that they will be heard for their many words. Do not be like them, for your Father knows what you need before you ask him. Pray then like this. Our Father in Heaven . . . "[6]

This simple P.R.A.Y.E.R. acrostic is inspired by the prayers of Jesus and will be helpful in your quest to achieve effective, relational and meaningful prayer:

- Praise: Worship God for who He is, what He has done, and what He will do
- Repent: Confess your sins and ask God to help you change
- Ask for Others: Intercede for the needs of others to help you stay outward focused
- Yourself: Ask the Lord to help you in your struggles and guide your future steps
- Express Thanks: Communicate how grateful you are for God's blessings
- Reflect: Be quiet and listen

George Mueller is known for a life of prayer and trusting God to provide food and finances for over 10,000 children sheltered in his orphanages in England. When George was in his eighties, a group of seminary students approached him and asked, "Mr. Mueller, what is your secret?" He pushed his chair back and began to bend his old limbs to the floor as he knelt in prayer. "This," George said. "This is the secret."

Prayer didn't come easy to me, but I caught on by watching my parents. My dad always found or made a "secret place" to pray in his home or church. Mom is sweet and soft-spoken with a gentle spirit, but she transforms into a mighty prayer warrior through the anointing of God's divine authority. Praying with perseverance is a legacy. I wasn't given an urn of ashes from a grandparent, but I was given a small two-by-two-foot prayer quilt. Its history is a powerful reminder and example.

Near the turn of the century in the early 1900s, my great-grandmother prayed for a new church to start in her community. After getting sore knees from kneeling on a wooden floor, she made a small prayer quilt to kneel upon. God answered her prayers. Her daughter, Velma, became a church planter with her husband, James. My Paw Paw and Gran became bi-vocational church planters in towns located in eastern Texas like Bloomington and Devil's Pocket. Gran passed down that same prayer quilt to my mom, who helped start new churches in Texas, New Hampshire, and Wisconsin. She made a wooden case with a glass window on top for this special family heirloom. I valued the quilt and the story, but I valued the prayers most of all. When my daughter Hannah Grace revealed God's calling on her life to be a missionary, my mom and I gave her the prayer quilt. Five generations of ministers are an answer to my great-grandmother's prayers.

You never know how far-reaching your prayers may be today. Your greatest gift to your friends and family is a strong prayer life. Leave a legacy for your children and friends. Nothing will keep your heart more tender for the Lord and others. When you pray, you become sensitive to the Holy Spirit, and your mind and heart aligns with the mind and heart of Christ. There will be times when you won't know how to pray for a matter. "Likewise the Spirit helps us in our weakness. For we do not know what to pray for as we ought, but the Spirit himself intercedes for us with groaning too deep for words" (Romans 8:26). This is an opportunity to pray in the Spirit and then pray with understanding. Praying in a spiritual and supernatural language will give you power and direction.

God gives you wisdom, and often the will of God is revealed through prayer. "Call to me and I will answer you, and will tell you great and hidden things that you have not known" (Jeremiah

33:3). Imagine if you spent more time asking God to reveal solutions to your future that you couldn't solve on your own.

Prayer can be more than a conversation. You can take it deeper by fasting. This ancient practice is one of the most neglected spiritual disciplines of the modern Church. It is powerful because it's doing without physically so that God can supernaturally do more. Jesus didn't say *if* you fast; He said *when.* "And when you fast, do not look gloomy like the hypocrites, for they disfigure their faces that their fasting may be seen by others. Truly, I say to you, they have received their reward. But when you fast, anoint your head and wash your face that your fasting may not be seen by others but by your Father who is in secret. And your Father who sees in secret will reward you."[7] If it's important to Jesus, it should be important to you.

Are you struggling with an obstacle? Do you need guidance? Is a friend or family member in need of some serious intercession? Ask the Holy Spirit to guide you in a fast. How that fast looks is between you and God. Most people think of food or drink when they think of fasting, but God can call you to fast from anything. What do you depend upon most? What do you devote the most time to? What hurts the inner heart the most when you think about giving it up for a time? Ask the Holy Spirit how much time you should block out to spend praying and reading Scripture rather than enjoying social media, food, or television.

One month before we started Gateway, I became aware of how much I needed God. It would never work without Him.[8] I was desperate for His power to accomplish what I knew I alone couldn't. While seeking His guidance and direction, I felt the Holy Spirit lead me to an extended fast for one month without food. Liquids only. It created an intense dependence upon Him for everything. It was hard and even painful at times, but it was also a sweet time of fellowship with my Lord Jesus. Through that fast, I learned to pray by the Spirit and pray with understanding.[9] God gave me more power, more grace, and a clearer vision than I ever had before. It pulled away the calluses of living a comfortable, physical life and made me sensitive to God and what mattered most to Him: His lost souls.[10]

A word of caution. These spiritual disciplines are in vain without love.[11] Jesus loved you first. When you remember and meditate on His great love for you, you will find yourself loving Him in return. Don't fast for others' praise or to add another notch to your spiritual belt. Fast as a pouring out of yourself.[12]

CORPORATE PRAYER

Group prayer is a powerful work for God. It brings unity through common focus. Jesus says if you agree in prayer with others concerning anything you ask, He will grant it.[13] Praying with others helps you keep prayers aligned with God's will. Praying with others will keep you humble. You are commanded to confess your sins to each other and pray so that you can be healed. If you consistently pray like this, you will have greater power and produce wonderful results.[14]

Prayer is hard work, but you must never give up. Persistent prayers by God's people cultivate a dependence upon God and a persevering spirit. Sometimes He waits to see how serious you are in prayer before blessing you with a solution. Your persistence reveals grit and a determination that touches the heart of God.

Are you willing to keep knocking, to keep seeking?[15] Jesus tells a parable as an example to help you not give up.

> In a certain city there was a judge who neither feared God nor respected man. And there was a widow in that city who kept coming to him and saying, "Give me justice against my adversary."
>
> For a while he refused, but afterward he said to himself, "Though I neither fear God nor respect man, yet because this widow keeps bothering me, I will give her justice, so that she will not beat me down by her continual coming."
>
> And the Lord said, "Hear what the unrighteous judge says. And will not God give justice to his elect, who cry to him day and night? Will he delay long over them? I tell you, he will give justice to them speedily. Nevertheless, when the Son of Man comes, will he find faith on earth?" (Luke 18:1–8)

Never quit. Your Father in heaven is listening. He is waiting. He says, "Ask of Me."[16] Change your prayer life from being "need focused" to "faith focused." God will answer prayers when you don't give up. It might take three weeks or three years or three decades. Trust in God and trust His timing. God's delay is not His denial. Pray together with your spouse, children, and friends. Ask how you can specifically pray for them and then pray out loud right then.

Never be timid or lazy in prayer. Be bold and discover the power of God. The author of Hebrews encourages you to finish your race with a "drawing near" that can only be achieved through prayer: "Let us then with confidence draw near to the throne of grace, that we may receive mercy and find grace to help in time of need."[17] You can't cross the finish line of your faith by yourself, but you can finish strong if you pray.

19

AMIGOS

SHADRACH, MESHACH, and ABEDNEGO

You are the average of the five people
you spend the most time with.

Jim Rohn

"You have cancer."

With those three words, Chris Campbell's life changed forever. A Chronic Myeloid Leukemia diagnosis should have stopped him—thirty-five and a father of four—in his tracks and crushed any dreams of the future. The diagnosis meant taking an astronomically expensive, targeted chemotherapy pill every day for the rest of his life, which caused a whole host of unpredictable and painful side effects. It meant regular doctor's visits, painful bone marrow biopsies, monthly blood drawing, and nail-biting days of waiting for results.

But my friend didn't let it stop him. Instead of slipping into despair, he clung to the Lord even more, surrendering all in broken submission. Every moment became even more precious. Many things were revealed to be weights holding him and his family back. The Lord used the trial to bring into sharp focus the vision He'd placed in his heart years before: the vision to plant a church.

Soon after the diagnosis, Campbell resigned from his job as a high school math teacher and joined our staff at Gateway in preparation to become a church planter. A few months later, the two of us and a handful of other staff members embarked on a climb to summit Mount Quandary, one of Colorado's fourteeners. The obstacles and mind games that crop up during extreme physical exertion and elevation changes like the ones Campbell faced on Mount Quandary served as important metaphors for ministry. It was a test to see if he was ready physically to church plant, and it would also grant him the opportunity to overcome the real physical restraints of cancer in miraculous fashion.

Before dawn, we left the trailhead in the dark at 5:45 a.m. in good spirits. But four hours later and only two-thirds of the way up, Campbell was drained. We all took turns carrying his backpack while feeding him energy bars and water. During the technical parts and sections of freehand rock climbing, we gently guided him by placing a steadying hand on his lower back for support.

It was brutal for him. But thirteen months after hearing the worst news of his life, Campbell summited his first fourteener. Standing on the peak before the breathtaking view, he called his wife in jubilant celebration with uncontrollable tears pouring down his face at the hard-won victory. They wept together over the miracle of God's power in the face of giants.

At some point on the way down, Campbell confessed, "I would have given up if you guys weren't with me." The challenge took everything my friend had emotionally, physically, and spiritually. It also made him accept help from others and rely on the Lord and his friends as a team in a way he never had before.

Teamwork and carrying burdens is fulfilling the law of Christ.[1] Jesus prayed we would be one as He and the Father are one.[2] He called us to love each other with His supernatural love and lay down our lives for our friends.[3] I think because of this spiritual DNA, my absolute favorite endurance events are team oriented like the "Tough Mudder," which I had the honor of finishing as part of a team with four soldiers. My experience of competing alongside these men was eye opening. With a combined thirty-one tours of overseas deployment, they understood the value of depending on brothers. During that race, they lived out the code to never leave anyone behind. Your faith marathon is not a solo event. The enemy will try to isolate you, but you need the right friends to help you finish strong.

Hebrews 11 mentions a group of friends who, by their faith, "quenched the power of fire." The author is probably referring to Shadrach, Meshach, and Abednego. These brave men refused to bow to King Nebuchadnezzar's image. As a result, they were thrown into a fiery furnace so hot that it killed the soldiers who pushed them in. Moments later, King Nebuchadnezzar witnessed a miracle that would change his life forever: "But I see four men unbound, walking in the midst of the fire, and they are not hurt; and the appearance of the fourth is like a son of the gods."[4] During the trial of a fiery furnace, this tight squad had each other plus one. They were not alone. Your squad plus Jesus is true, biblical fellowship.

If Jesus belonged to a small group by living with twelve disciples for three years, you should too. Church is not a building; it's people. Scripture describes this fellowship of believers with relational terms: "flock," "family," "body," "bride." Some would say you only need Jesus, but why would you just desire the head when you could have the whole body? Others prefer the safety of isolation because they've been hurt by believers. The truth is that the Church is imperfect because she is made up of imperfect people. This is no excuse for keeping others at arm's length and disobeying Scripture, which tells us to never neglect meeting together.[5] The Bible mentions the phrase "one another" fifty-nine times. Greet one another.[6] Honor one another and be devoted to one another.[7] Live in harmony with one another.[8] Serve one another.[9] Be kind to one another.[10] Forgive one another.[11] Love one another.[12] This last one is mentioned the most!

You need to receive and give love. It's impossible to fulfill the teachings and commands of Jesus without being in community. It's like marriage. No marriage is perfect. There will be hurt and conflict in marriage, but it's worth it in the long run if you can forgive, stick it out, and be faithful as the Lord has remained faithful and forgiving to you. No doubt about it. You need others and they need you. "Two are better than one, because they have a good reward for their toil. For if they fall, one will lift up his fellow. But woe to him who is alone when he falls and has not another to lift him up!"[13] You need a squad of healthy, Christian relationships.

The friends you choose to be in your inner circle will determine your destiny. Show me your friends and I'll show you your future. Friends will bring you up or tear you down. Isolation and toxic friendships will prevent you from finishing your race. They'll cling to you like dead weight. There are few things more deadly than a toxic friend.

Some historians believe the term "dead weight" comes from a famous epic poem called the *Aeneid*. Penned by Virgil, a Roman philosopher who died a few decades before the birth of Jesus, it records a horrifying execution practiced by the Romans at that time where a corpse was tied to a living body, hand on hand and face-to-face. The corpse in this deadly embrace would quickly release toxic chemicals, poisonous fumes, and deadly bodily fluids that would kill the living person through a lingering, tortuous death that sometimes lasted days. The *Aeneid* was to the Romans what Homer's *Odyssey* and *Iliad* were to the Greeks, so it was a well-known piece of literature. Paul even possibly referred to it as a spiritual example at the end of Romans 7: "Who will save me from this body of death?"

Don't let bad company take you down a spiraling, spiritual death. Make the tough decision to free yourself from unhealthy relationships even if the people you share them with are believers. Ask yourself, do we drive each other closer to holiness and the Lord, or do we share the same weaknesses and act as a poison to each other? My friend and golf coach at the University of Texas at San Antonio, John Knauer, has a motto: "Life is too short and the van is too small to keep a turd on the team."

Finishers have authentic friends who passionately love Jesus. They may not have many, but they are real. They finish because they've discovered the value of a small group as a safe place to be vulnerable and fight for each other in the real battles, in the grit and the grime of life. A lot of people don't believe Jesus is real because they don't see Christians *being* real. Start by sharing your story with your trusted inner circle of genuine friends who you can stay intentional with and see how God turns your junk into evangelistic gold.

My squad is known as the "Five Amigos." It became the title name of our group text. We are all from Texas and met each other in high school or college. Coincidentally, Texas comes from the Spanish word *tejas*, which means "friend." I treasure my buddies Matt, Rusty, Darrell, and Brian. I strongly believe one of the reasons we are all still in ministry is because of our friendship. For the last several years, a day has not gone by when I'm not encouraged, prayed for, or laughed at by one of my amigos. Nobody gets too high or too low. We often carve out a trip or two every year so that our families can spend time together as well. If you want these kinds of friends, start by demonstrating these valuable attributes to others. Be a friend who is loyal, fun, encouraging, honest, and unselfish.

LOYAL

Love protects. "A friend loves at all times, and a brother is born for adversity."[14] Be the friend who would have someone's back during good times and bad. After the Battle of Kasserine Pass in 1943, United States troops adopted the modern foxhole, a vertical hole in the ground deep enough for two soldiers to stand back-to-back in with only their heads and shoulders exposed. Be a deeply dug, foxhole friend who will drop everything to be back-to-back with your buddy in a fight. Be there when he is at his best and worst. Know when to ask the tough questions in private and always be loyal in public. Be faithful and committed no matter what others say about your friend.

FUN

Love and laughter plow hearts. "A joyful heart is good medicine."[15] Be a friend who easily laughs at yourself and laughs often with your friends. Allow the bond of trust to become like glue through the fellowship of meals and trips. Be the first to celebrate without envy. Share stories and memories often.

ENCOURAGING

Build up with your words. "Iron sharpens iron, and one man sharpens another."[16] It's essential for your squad to be a safe place where others can be themselves without fear of judgment. When a need is shared with you, take it seriously, actively listen with your heart, and pray. Allow the Holy Spirit to guide you if there is a need to encourage. Often your presence, listening ear, and prayers will be enough. Check back in to see how your friend is doing. Not carrying your friend's burden is disobedience to Christ.[17] Be a dependable shoulder for him or her to lean on. Be known as a positive encourager instead of a fault finder. Be a friend who keeps no record of wrongs. Believe the best.[18] Get the extra rep out of your friend even when he doesn't think he can lift the weight one more time. Be a support system when needed.

HONEST

An honest friend is a trusted friend. "Faithful are the wounds of a friend; profuse are the kisses of an enemy."[19] Jesus was full of grace and truth,[20] and we should be too. Grace says I love you no matter what. Truth says I must be honest with you no matter what. Be willing to have tough conversations when needed.

UNSELFISH

Kyle and I had never surfed a day in our lives. We borrowed boards and paddled out into the deep, green-brown Gulf of Mexico off the coast of Mustang Island. The waves never get big in that location, so how difficult could it be? We never even had the chance to stand up on our boards because an unexpected riptide took us further out into the ocean, far beyond the safety of the shallows. We didn't panic but knew things were serious. My triathlon training provided enough strength for me to paddle against the tide, toward shore. I was safe, but as I looked back I noticed my friend was not. Kyle was exhausted.

I made the decision to go back and help. I attached our boards with a small rope, but I was not strong enough to paddle myself and pull him on his board. After several minutes of struggle, we didn't give up and kept on. Our jokes about needing the Coast Guard subsided when we realized the real threat of being out in the ocean at night. With sharks. I can't tell you how much better the situation was by having each other.

Our last chance of salvation came in a glimpse of a rock jetty in the distance. We made the decision to paddle hard in a diagonal toward it. When we got close, we abandoned our boards to launch ourselves onto the rugged rocks that were covered in jagged crustaceans and barnacles. We shredded the skin on the bottoms of our feet climbing over those cheese graters, but it was all good because we were safe.

In friendship, you reap what you sow. Kyle may not have had experience in swimming, but what he'd learned through white water canoeing paid off. One morning in March, during an annual, early spring rain that is common in the Texas Hill Country when rivers are at peak height, Kyle and I braved the frigid water of the Guadalupe River to go canoeing together. When the white water appeared, Kyle would yell, "Keep paddling!" from the rear lead position of the canoe to keep us on line. When I fell out, Kyle helped me pull myself back in.

A large cycling group is known as a peloton. Riding in a peloton is valuable because it offers protection and efficiency. When you ride solo you are isolated and at risk of being hit by a vehicle. If you get into an accident or have a mechanical failure, who will help you? Riding in a peloton not only offers protection, it is also more fun. Taking turns in the lead helps the others by drafting behind the leader. Find your peloton.

Belong to a small group. Treasure your squad. Together, you'll be unstoppable if you never let each other down. Be generous with your time, words, and resources. "A man of many companions may come to ruin, but there is a friend who sticks closer than a brother."[21] Jesus says there is no greater love than to lay down your life for your friends.[22] Love is sacrificial. It constantly places the needs of your friends above your own. Be intentional because life is short and at the end of the race, who you cross the finish line with is what will matter most.

20

THE FINISH LINE

YOU

What you do today could affect
where others spend eternity.

Dwain Jones

The Travis Letter, a world-renowned historical document largely considered the most heroic letter ever written, was inspired in a church. As the smell of gunpowder, blast of cannons, and crack of rifles filled the air, twenty-six-year-old Lieutenant Colonel William B. Travis wrote an open letter within the besieged walls of a mission called the Alamo. Surrounded and outnumbered seven to one, the Texans' only hope for survival was reinforcements. Just one week before Washington delegates declared the independence of Texas and eleven days prior to his tragic, courageous death, Travis penned this letter and made history.

> Commandancy of the Alamo
> Bejar, Feby. 24th. 1836
>
> To the People of Texas & All Americans in the World

Fellow Citizens and Compatriots:

I am besieged, by a thousand or more of the Mexicans under Santa Anna. I have sustained a continual Bombardment & cannonade for 24 hours & have not lost a man. The enemy has demanded a surrender at discretion, otherwise, the garrison are to be put to the sword, if the fort is taken. I have answered the demand with a cannon shot, & our flag still waves proudly from the walls. I shall never surrender or retreat. Then, I call on you in the name of Liberty, of patriotism & everything dear to the American character, to come to our aid, with all dispatch. The enemy is receiving reinforcements daily & will no doubt increase to three or four thousand in four or five days. If this call is neglected, I am determined to sustain myself as long as possible & die like a soldier who never forgets what is due to his own honor & that of his country—VICTORY OR DEATH.

William Barret Travis.
Lt. Col. comdt.

P.S. The Lord is on our side. When the enemy appeared in sight we had not three bushels of corn. We have since found in deserted houses 80 or 90 bushels and got into the walls 20 or 30 head of Beeves.

Travis

Though the Battle of the Alamo did nothing to aid the Texas Revolution from a military standpoint and the 250 soldiers under Travis's command did not survive, the Alamo provided a powerful story of fearlessness and resolve in the face of almost certain death that left a far deeper impression on history than anyone could have imagined at the time. "Remember the Alamo!" became a war cry that symbolized everything Americans stood for. General Santa Anna, the leader of the Mexican forces, meant to psychologically pulverize the resolve of the Texans. Instead the Alamo became a rallying cry that led the Texan army to victory less than two months after Travis wrote the letter. Historians theorize it is likely that the battle would have been won or a ceasefire would have been reached if Travis's plea for reinforcements had been answered in time.

There is another plea for brave reinforcements for a cause and Kingdom that matters far more, and, like in the Battle of the Alamo, time is of the essence.[1] There are many who would prefer a comfortable life exempt from danger and problems. Quitting early is a guarantee you'll never experience what God desires to do through your life. Will you play it safe or be one of the faithful who endures hardship for the cause of Christ? Will you "Remember the Cross!" as the Texans remembered the Alamo? Even if the Lord calls you to run your race in the face of mortal danger, remember what Jesus said in Matthew 10:39: "Whoever loses his life for My sake will find it." In Jesus, death is swallowed up in victory and it has lost its sting.[2] Others run for a wreath that will fade and be forgotten, but we run for an imperishable wreath, one that not even death can take away.[3]

The "great cloud of witnesses" the author of Hebrews lists in chapter 11 is the group of other endurance runners who answered the call for reinforcements and finished strong even when persecuted unto death. They did not achieve "victory or death" but victory in death!

> Others suffered mocking and flogging, and even chains and imprisonment. They were stoned, they were sawn in two, they were killed with the sword. They went about in skins of sheep and goats, destitute, afflicted, mistreated—of whom the world was not worthy—wandering about in deserts and mountains, and in dens and caves of the earth. And all these, though commended through their faith, did not receive what was promised, since God had provided something better for us, that apart from us they should not be made perfect (Hebrews 11:36–40).

ANSWER THE CALL

Unreached people are waiting for someone to bring them the good news, the Gospel of Jesus Christ. The call is great, but few are even listening. Most western churches are in decline. The solution is discipleship. None of the following are acceptable excuses: selfishness, laziness, disobedience, and fear. One day when you stand before the Throne, the excuses that seemed good to you now will crumble before the holy righteousness of the Lord. Are video games and Netflix worth not hearing, "Well done, good and faithful servant"?[4] Entertainment can't get more time than the Kingdom. Your great opportunity, the calling Jesus gave us all, is to make disciples.[5] Jesus' method of relationally sacrificing is still the best way. Who are we to say we know a better way?

God is calling faithful, available, and teachable servants. He is looking for those with passion who will finish as well as they began. He is looking for those who will say yes. Selfishly disobeying the great commission of Jesus to go and make disciples may seem nice at first. Your talent will be buried in the ground and the enemy won't hound you because you're not a threat.[6]

If all is well in your life, perhaps it's time to search your heart and re-evaluate your actions. There is no such thing as neutrality in the war for souls. Nothing in nature remains as it is; it is either growing or dying. Which are you? Your inaction will not only harm you and those around you (bad company corrupts),[7] it will also be a slap in the face to the cloud of witnesses, to those who suffered greatly so you could receive the baton of faith. The Lord calls out to you. Receive the baton and honor the endurance runners of the past who sacrificed so much for you. Will you now pass it on to others in great need of the Gospel?

The harvest is here, but the workers are few. Others who came before you and others who live now are obeying the Lord's command to pray for more laborers.[8] Will you be an answer to those prayers? Your Lord Jesus Christ says, "As the Father has sent me, even so I am sending you" (John 20:21). You cross the finish line when you obey the command, the call to be sent. How you run your race can echo for eternity.

Jesus commands you to store up treasure in heaven, for where your treasure is so will your heart be.[9] Give yourself to the advancement of God's Kingdom. Surrender to God's purposes. Hold lightly to the things in this world. "But I do not account my life of any value nor as precious to myself, if only I may finish my course and the ministry that I received from the Lord Jesus, to testify to the gospel of the grace of God" (Acts 20:24).

The calling to make disciples is for every follower of Jesus. It supersedes place and occupation. God desires to use your experience and education in your workplace. Every believer should be a missionary, every Christian parent should be a pastor. Your first church is the family in your home, and your first mission field is your place of work. The Lord is looking to build an army of valiant, humble, faithful soldiers who can share His good news with His people.

He needs some to be sent and some to stay. Some to intercede in prayer, others to generously give, encourage, and support or go as short-term missionaries. Where you are is where you testify. It is all important and spiritual. If God has not given you inner conviction for full-time ministry, don't allow anyone to make you feel guilty. You are vital to His plan and needed right where you are.

The Lord used one stay-at-home mom to change the world. Her name was Susanna Wesley, the mother of John and Charles Wesley. These men were world-changing evangelists and founders of the Methodist Church. Susanna is revered in Church history for her formational work in her sons. Don't devalue what you do. God is the only One who can bring value and holiness, and He is with you. He makes you valuable and holy on this Earth and no one can take that away. You can, however, squander God's investment.

So what if God is calling you to go into full-time ministry? He will give you a growing sense of dissatisfaction for anything else. When it becomes as important as breathing, nothing will stop you. He may even give you a burning passion for the ministry so that you may "lead with zeal." He will also call you through an inner compass of peace, Scripture, and wise counsel to confirm this direction. God will orchestrate many things beyond the possibility of coincidence. Wait on Him. No matter the pressure, don't try to cross the Red Sea before He parts the water. You'll know when it's time.

Will you love Jesus and His lost children enough to obey? Will you maximize where God has positioned you as an ambassador to this world for His glory? Will you sacrifice to bring the good news of Jesus to unreached places even if they're only within your home? Will you join a church planting team in places of great need? Will you surrender comforts and riches for the clarion call to go and make disciples of all nations? When you do, set it in your mind to never quit until you cross that finish line and surrender your will to the Lord.

EXECUTE FAITH

Your mission is simple: Help your friends become devoted followers of Jesus. When you answer the call of Jesus, your faith will be amplified when you become aware of His continual presence and power through the Holy Spirit. You will never experience the adventure and joy of making disciples until you abide in Him. And you will never experience spiritual growth until you take spiritual responsibility for others.

Start now. Take what has been invested in you and submit yourself to training to become a small group leader. If God is calling you to be a missionary, start with your neighbor and invite her over for a meal. If God is calling you to be a church planter, start with your friend who sits near you in class. If God is calling you to full-time ministry, start by sharing your story of faith with your co-worker. Bloom where you are planted. Never give up.

By faith, you will take your first step. By faith, you will not hit the panic button when you are rejected or face danger. By faith, you will not grow weary when you remember the unchanging character of Jesus and His unshakable Kingdom.[10] By faith, you will be bold as a lion.[11] By faith, you will trust in the Lord when you witness unjust suffering. By faith, you will not be moved.

EXPECT SUFFERING

Religious liberties are being stripped away daily all over the world. Standing firm with biblical convictions contrary to the shifting cultural standards will result in persecution. Jesus was persecuted on His way to the cross and asks you to bear the same pain for His sake. He says to "count the cost"[12] and "take up your cross."[13] This means contemplating the suffering before you. Pretending there will be no opposition ahead does you no favors. Scripture says, "through many tribulations we must enter the kingdom of God."[14]

Jesus tells you to expect persecution if you live your life aligned with the nature and purposes of God. He promises in the final beatitude, "Blessed are those who are persecuted for righteousness' sake, for theirs is the kingdom of heaven. Blessed are you when others revile you and persecute you and utter all kinds of evil against you falsely on my account. Rejoice and be glad, for your reward is great in heaven, for so they persecuted the prophets who were before you."[15] Scripture tells us what will happen to you when you live as Jesus did. "Beloved, do not be surprised at the fiery trial when it comes upon you to test you, as though something strange were happening to you."[16] Don't stop when things get tough. Aren't you glad Jesus didn't?

FINISH STRONG

You have everything you need to cross the finish line. In his benediction to the Hebrew Christians, the apostle writes, "Now may the God of peace who brought again from the dead our Lord Jesus, the great shepherd of the sheep, by the blood of the eternal covenant, equip you with everything good that you may do His will, working in us that which is pleasing in His sight, through Jesus Christ, to whom be glory forever and ever. Amen."[17]

Although I didn't feel great about my training, I said yes to an endurance event called the Tall Texan Tri. This half IRONMAN took place in Boerne, Texas, in the middle of the intense summer heat. After swimming a mile in a lake and cycling fifty-two miles, I hit the wall during the run with only three miles to the finish line. At that moment, I looked ahead to see a giant hill where many runners sat on the side of the road. I didn't want to continue, but I noticed a familiar car at the base of the climb. There in the distance, a man waved his hand. He wasn't a competitor in the race, but he also wasn't just any spectator. He was my dad. As I ran closer, he jumped out of the car, cheering as he ran along beside me, "You can do it, son. You only have three miles left. I believe in you. You're not alone in this."

Your Father in heaven is saying this to you now. Can you hear him?

I need you. My Church will finish this race. The gates of hell will not prevail.[18] I want you to be a part of what is happening. These are the most exciting times. Go out sprinting for the finish line with grit in your mouth, burned lungs, and bruised feet. You won't regret it. There must be new ways and methods of starting new churches. Will you be a part of this mission? Will you take the baton? Will you take up the machete and go into the jungle to make a new way? Go for it. It must not end with you. Don't back down to anyone or anything. Never look back. For he who does is not fit for my Kingdom.[19]

Will you obey and endure the calling to go? Will you be able to declare like the apostle Paul, "I have fought the good fight, I have finished the race, I have kept the faith"?[20] Will you finish your race? It's your turn. Dig deep. Map out your course and run it with the enduring faith given to you by your Lord Jesus Christ.

By faith, I will, and you will too.

FREE ONLINE RESOURCES

TO UNLOCK FREE RESOURCES, VISIT THE *MARATHON FAITH* WEBSITE at www.MarathonFaith.org. Use the code marathonfaith2819 to access discussion questions for small groups, videos, sermons, and a training program for a 5k.

ACKNOWLEDGMENTS

Mandy Campbell: Thank you for your unwavering guidance as my writing coach.

Gary Terashita: I'll always be grateful for you seeking me out and believing in me as my editor.

Karen Dunavan: Thank you for your attention to detail that ensured every "i" had a dot and every "t" was crossed.

Stephanie Van Pay: This would never have happened without your support and blessing. I love you.

NOTES

ONE: LOOK WHERE YOU WANT TO GO

1. John 17:3.

TWO: DIE DAILY

1. Dietrich Bonhoeffer, *The Cost of Discipleship* (New York: Macmillan, 1961).

THREE: WALK WITH GOD

1. Hebrews 12:1b.
2. 2 Timothy 4:7.
3. John 15:4.
4. John 6:51.
5. Genesis 5:24.
6. Matthew 20:28.
7. John 17:21, 24.
8. Brother Lawrence, *The Practice of the Presence of God* (Rockville, MD: Wildside Press, 2010).
9. Hebrews 12:1.

10. Jeremiah 29:12–13.
11. Matthew 5:6.
12. 1 Peter 2:2.
13. John 4:14.
14. John 6:55.
15. Mark 1:35.
16. Matthew 6:6.
17. Psalm 46:10.
18. Wayne Cordeiro, *The Divine Mentor* (Minneapolis: Bethany House Publishers, 2008).
19. Psalm 119:11; Joshua 1:8; Isaiah 55:11.
20. John 15:4–7.
21. 1 Corinthians 16:13.
22. Matthew 4:1–11.
23. Proverbs 7:3.
24. 1 Peter 2:2; 2 Timothy 3:16; 1 Corinthians 10:13.
25. Revelation 2:2–4.
26. Hebrews 12:2; Revelation 22:13.

FOUR: SWING THAT HAMMER

1. Genesis 6:5.
2. Genesis 6:17.
3. Proverbs 29:18, KJV.
4. Matthew 24:21.
5. Matthew 10:28.
6. Psalm 132:14.
7. Genesis 6:9.
8. James 2:17.
9. W. Kyle Volkmer, *These Things: A Reference Manual for Discipleship* (San Antonio: The Passionate Few, 2016).
10. Luke 2:49.
11. Mark 10:45.
12. 1 Corinthians 9:24–27, MSG.
13. 1 Peter 2:9.

14. Ephesians 6:12; 1 Corinthians 10:3–4.
15. Philippians 3:20.
16. 2 Peter 3:7.

FIVE: BETTER TOGETHER

1. Genesis 17:17.
2. Genesis 22:2.
3. Hebrews 11:1.
4. Genesis 15:5, 22:17–18.
5. Hebrews 11:19.
6. Genesis 15:6.
7. Matthew 20:25–28; Ephesians 5:25; 28–29.
8. Ephesians 5:25–32.
9. Matthew 22: 36–40.
10. Craig Groeschel, *Confessions of a Pastor: Adventures in Dropping the Pose and Getting Real with God* (Colorado Springs: Multnomah, 2006).

SIX: PASS THE BATON

1. Proverbs 27:1; James 4:14–15.
2. Genesis 27:26–29; 39–40.
3. Genesis 25:29–34.
4. Genesis 3:15.
5. Genesis 22:18.
6. Genesis 15:20.
7. Proverbs 13:24; Hebrews 12:6–11.
8. Romans 12:2.
9. Ephesians 4:14.
10. Psalm 19:7.
11. Mountains over 14,000 feet in height.
12. Scripture, Observation, Application, and Prayer.
13. Luke 15:11–32.

SEVEN: FIGHT

1. Genesis 49:33.
2. Genesis 47:31.
3. Matthew 7:7.
4. Philippians 2:12.
5. 1 Corinthians 9:25.
6. Joshua 5:14.
7. 1 Samuel 17:47.
8. Genesis 3:9.
9. Genesis 4:10.
10. John 8:11; Romans 8:1.
11. Helen Howarth Lemmel, "Turn Your Eyes upon Jesus," https://hymnary.org/text/o_soul_are_you_weary_and_troubled.
12. James 4:7.
13. Matthew 4:1–11.
14. 2 Timothy 4:7–8.

EIGHT: TRIALS POSSESS GREAT PURPOSE

1. Hebrews 11:1.
2. John 16:33.
3. Romans 8:17; 1 Peter 2:21; Mark 9:34; 1 Peter 4:13.
4. Isaiah 55:11; Philippians 1:6.
5. Hebrews 12:2.
6. Hebrews 12:11.
7. Isaiah 40:31.
8. Philippians 4:7.
9. 1 John 5:4.
10. 2 Corinthians 12:5; Galatians 6:14.
11. E. Stanley Jones, *Christ and Human Suffering* (Nashville: Abingdon Press, 1933).
12. Galatians 6:2.

NINE: BE BRAVE

1. Hebrews 11:23.

2. J. R. R. Tolkien, *The Two Towers* (London: George Allen & Unwin Ltd., 1954).
3. James 2:19.

ELEVEN: ALL IN

1. Garth Stein, *The Art of Racing in the Rain* (New York: Harper, 2008).
2. William Shakespeare, *Julius Caesar*, Act 2, Scene 2.
3. John J. Pullen, *Joshua Chamberlain: A Hero's Life and Legacy* (Mechanicsburg, PA: Stackpole Books, 1999).
4. Romans 2:11; Galatians 3:28.
5. Hebrews 10:38.

TWELVE: DROP THE DEAD WEIGHT

1. Matthew 7:5.
2. Romans 14.
3. Andy Stanley, *Choosing to Cheat: Who Wins When Family and Work Collide?* (New York: Multnomah, 2003).
4. Proverbs 22:7.
5. John 15:5.
6. Matthew 14:13–21.
7. Romans 12:8.
8. Philippians 4:6–9.

THIRTEEN: DON'T LET SUCCESS GET TO YOUR HEAD

1. Lance Armstrong, *It's Not About the Bike—My Journey Back to Life* (New York: Berkley Books, 2001).
2. Daniel 5:24–28.
3. Isaiah 55:8–9.
4. 1 Samuel 15.
5. 1 Kings 11:1–8.
6. John 14:6.
7. Andrew Murray, *Humility* (Create Space Independent Publishing Platform, 2014).

8. Pat Summitt, *Reach for the Summit: The Definite Dozen System for Succeeding at Whatever You Do* (New York: Crown Business, 1999).

FOURTEEN: DON'T LET FAILURE GET TO YOUR HEART

1. "For Demas, in love with this present world, has deserted me and gone to Thessalonica" (2 Timothy 4:10).
2. Judges 16:19.
3. Judges 16:22.
4. Judges 16:23–27.
5. Judges 16:28–30.
6. Proverbs 24:16.
7. Jeremiah 29:11.
8. Hebrews 12:5–11.
9. Ephesians 2:10.
10. Matthew 5:4.
11. Hebrews 4:14–16.
12. Romans 5:12–21; Colossians 1:15.
13. Luke 17:1.
14. Psalm 147:3.
15. Genesis 50:20.
16. 2 Corinthians 5:17.

FIFTEEN: GRIT

1. Proverbs 27:6.
2. 1 Peter 5:10.
3. Zechariah 4:10.
4. Deuteronomy 23:2.
5. Judges 11:3.
6. Mariano Rivera, *The Closer* (New York: Little, Brown and Company, 2014).
7. Nazareth is located in lower Galilee.
8. John 7:52; John 1:46.

9. Mark 6:4.
10. 1 Timothy 4:12.
11. Romans 2:11.
12. Acts 2:17–18.
13. Matthew 28:20; Isaiah 54:5; John 1:12.
14. 1 Corinthians 1:27.
15. Judges 11:14–27.
16. David Livingston, *The Life and African Exploration of David Livingstone* (New York: Cooper Square Press, 2002).
17. Matthew 25:23.

SIXTEEN: CONSTANT FORGIVENESS

1. This name has been changed.
2. 1 Samuel 24:1–22.
3. Matthew 5:21–22; 1 John 3:15.
4. Ephesians 4:31–32.
5. Matthew 6:15.
6. Matthew 5:7.
7. 1 Corinthians 13.
8. 1 Corinthians 13.
9. Matthew 5:44, Luke 6:28.
10. Luke 23:34.
11. John 13:35.
12. John 13:27.

SEVENTEEN: REST TO BE YOUR BEST

1. 1 Samuel 3:10.
2. Exodus 18:13–26.
3. Ephesians 4:11–12.
4. Exodus 20:8.
5. Genesis 2:1–3.
6. Ed Stetzer, "How Protestant Pastors Spend Their Time," *The Exchange* (blog), December 29, 2009, http://www.christianitytoday.

com/edstetzer/2009/december/how-protestant-pastors-spend-their-time.html.
7. Luke 5:16.
8. Leviticus 25:1–55.

EIGHTEEN: PERSEVERING WITH PRAYER

1. Hebrews 11:33.
2. Daniel 6:10.
3. Daniel 6:20.
4. 1 Peter 5:8.
5. Luke 11:1.
6. Matthew 6:7–9.
7. Matthew 6:16–18.
8. Luke 18:27.
9. Romans 8:26–27.
10. Luke 19:10.
11. 1 Corinthians 13.
12. Romans 12:1; Matthew 6:16–18.
13. Matthew 18:19.
14. James 5:16.
15. Matthew 7:7.
16. Psalm 2:8.
17. Hebrews 4:16.

NINETEEN: AMIGOS

1. Galatians 6:2.
2. John 17:21–23.
3. John 34–35; 15:13.
4. Daniel 3:25.
5. Hebrews 10:25.
6. 2 Corinthians 13:12.
7. Romans 12:10.
8. Romans 12:16.
9. Galatians 5:13.

10. Ephesians 4:32.
11. Colossians 3:13.
12. John 15:12.
13. Ecclesiastes 4:9–10.
14. Proverbs 17:17.
15. Proverbs 17:22.
16. Proverbs 27:17.
17. Galatians 6:2.
18. 1 Corinthians 13:4–8.
19. Proverbs 27:6.
20. John 1:14.
21. Proverbs 18:24.
22. John 15:13.

TWENTY: THE FINISH LINE

1. Mark 13:35; 1 Thessalonians 5:6.
2. 1 Corinthians 15:54–55.
3. 1 Corinthians 9:25.
4. Matthew 25:21.
5. Matthew 28:19–20.
6. Matthew 25:18, 24–30.
7. 1 Corinthians 15:33.
8. Matthew 9:37–38.
9. Matthew 6:20.
10. Hebrews 12:18–29.
11. Proverbs 28:1.
12. Luke 14:28.
13. Matthew 16:24.
14. Acts 14:22.
15. Matthew 5:10–12.
16. 1 Peter 4:12.
17. Hebrews 13:20–21.
18. Matthew 16:18.

19. Luke 9:62.
20. 2 Timothy 4:7.